For three months, before going to bed, Leny M. Poetry. *Glimpses: A Poetic Memoir,* contains what emerged from her listening to what is to come in the sacredness of it all." The root of the word memoir—a kind of record, a memory—is cleverly positioned with poetry lines which begin with, "I forgot..." and which also serve as the catalyst for characteristically deep contemplations [her "holy tunganga" (gaze)], and the emergence of stories between forgetting and remembering again. Many of the pieces muse about learning: "learning that we are energy and consciousness"; "learning to tune in more closely to the scientific fact... that we are made of stars and stardust"—the attunements of a scholar and her deeply beautiful sensitivities toward nature's rhythms and message.
—**Lisa Suguitan Melnick, author of** *#30 Collantes Street*

As soon as I started reading Leny's journal entries, triggered as she puts it by Eileen Tabios' poems, I immediately felt I was in for an intimate journey with an old friend who has been a fount of wisdom through her own research, revelations and reflections. Her book, *Coming Full Circle,* opened my eyes that welled with tears when I realized for the first time why Filipinos believed they were doomed to fail, and how this insidious belief defined our outlook, making us feel small and inferior. Leny's latest book, *Glimpses: A Poetic Memoir,* reminds me yet again of the power of "indigenous consciousness," of recovering our memories, and of remembering and rewriting our stories. In this context, I am able to view past incidents and images in my life with a deeper understanding of my own history and what that means moving forward. Leny's honest and open evocations of her own truths as she crafts "a new way of being in the world," profoundly speak to me as I sort through my own encounters and entanglements, particularly as they relate to our shared passion of building community.
—**Jon Melegrito, Civil Rights Advocate and Editor-in-Chief of** *Manila Mail* **(Washington, D.C.)**

GLIMPSES provides an insightful, poetic journey into Leny Mendoza Strobel's memories, musings, reveries, impressions, perceptions, and inventions as encouraged by Eileen Tabios's MDR poetry generator. Journal entry for 4.3.18 struck a chord: "I forgot when memory became a colander with generous holes / And perhaps we need those big-holed colanders as sieves for unwanted memories of a broken past / But wait / Why call the past 'broken'? /...Sure the past reeks of colonial ventures that trampled islands and archipelagos / But we are still here / We have not been made to disappear /...Everything can be reframed / Stories can be edited /...I've been pondering this for a while now / I think of Tongva elder, L Frank, saying: They've taken nothing from us. We are still stardust / Remember your strength / Remember your Source / How do we tell this to each other?" Maraming salamat for sharing your heart with us. Yes, we are still stardust.
—**Abraham Ignacio, Librarian, Filipino American Center, San Francisco Public Library**

Liberating. Poetic. So beautiful that each page choked me with different emotions—love, pain, happiness, anger, hatred. She reminds me that wherever we are, our 'womanity' and the strength that we have inherited from our ancestors cannot be taken away from us. Through her poetic memoir, Dr. Strobel speaks to us through her beautifully and painfully woven experiences. And we can talk back. She has the answers. Dr. Strobel's journey mirrors the diaspora of a Filipino woman in search of the self and finding the self that has become stronger in a foreign land despite the struggles and questions. I read her words with my heart.

—Eunice Barbara C. Novio, educator, journalist, and recipient of the 2017 Plaridel Award, Philippine American Press Club

Taking another poet's lines as her starting points, Leny creates mediations and meditations within which she tells her story and invites her readers to come in and dwell a while to contemplate what she has created: a retreat, a cocoon, a place in which to see oneself and to be seen, from which to spin forward and inspire other poetic awakenings.

—Myriam J. A. Chancy, Guggenheim Fellow, author of *The Loneliness of Angels,* and HBA Chair in the Humanities, Scripps College

GLIMPSES

A Poetic Memoir

(Through the MDR Poetry Generator)

Leny Mendoza Strobel

Paloma Press, 2019

ISBN 978-1-7323025-8-7

Library of Congress Control Number: 2019932044

Cover art by Leny Mendoza Strobel

Book cover design by Perla Ramos Paredes, Omehra Sigahne

Interior Design by C. Sophia Ibardaloza

ALSO FROM PALOMA PRESS:

Blue by Wesley St. Jo & Remé Grefalda
Manhattan: An Archaeology by Eileen R. Tabios
Anne with an E & Me by Wesley St. Jo
Humors by Joel Chace
My Beauty is an Occupiable Space by Anne Gorrick & John Bloomberg-Rissman
peminology by Melinda Luisa de Jesús
Close Apart by Robert Cowan
One, Two, Three: Selected Hay(na)ku Poems by Eileen R. Tabios, translated into Spanish by Rebeka Lembo (Bilingual Edition)
HAY(NA)KU 15 edited by Eileen R. Tabios
HUMANITY, anthology edited by Eileen R. Tabios
The Great American Novel by Eileen R. Tabios
The Good Mother of Marseille by Christopher X. Shade
Diaspora Volume L by Ivy Alvarez
Elsewhen by Robert Cowan, illustrated by Ada Cowan

PALOMA PRESS
San Mateo & Morgan Hill, California
Publishing Poetry+Prose since 2016
www.palomapress.net

For Noah

CONTENTS

Foreword

Poetry asks: Must words be trapped by definitions?

That is one of the questions raised by my "MURDER DEATH RESURRECTION" (MDR) project.* Through MDR, I created a collection of 1,167 poetic lines by reading (at the time) 27 prior poetry collections. The concepts of "murder," "death," and "resurrection" were intended to symbolize how I was replacing (murdering and putting to death) the older poems with new (resurrected) poems. The resulting lines, as anticipated, veered off from the older poems' original contexts—the new lines had to reflect my changed identity years after writing the older poems, the new contexts imposed by changed times as well as memory lapses, and new considerations of the language.

One of MDR's intents, therefore, must be to show the fluidity of words—how they can mean, evoke, and call out different things from different readers and writers who use them. I'm honored that Leny M. Strobel was moved to use the MDR's poetry lines as impetus for new writing. When I published the MDR's lines, it was with the intent of having their readers create new poems and art as a result of reading them—just as I had created new poems from reading older poems.

First, Leny created new poems by randomly combining my poetry lines. Next, and as shown in this book, she created a memoir by writing each section as a "free-write" from a randomly-chosen line. Many of these surprise—their unexpected results are a gift to the writer. Don't we writers want to face new dimensions to our works as a result of readers? A Gift. Read how one of my entries, the line

> *"I forgot weeping over the language shared by a toddler and a stuffed animal"*

becomes one of Leny's brief memoirs ending with a sentence one could never anticipate from mine:

> *"Today, a German writer, Andreas Weber, calls these: Erotic encounters with the biosphere and geosphere."*

I could continue with so many examples. Instead, I invite you, Dear Reader to simply read Leny's own words—you need not read these dated free-writes chronologically; feel free to open the book at random—and marvel, as I did and do, over a life so richly- and well-lived.

You might also be moved to write in response to Leny's writings, for great writing often inspires readers to write as well. Such is the fluidity of words: they are not meant to be trapped in stasis. They can move beyond dictionary definitions and contexts defined by other authors to become directly applicable to your life. Such is Poetry's suggestion, and, to my and our gratitude, Leny's book is proof.

—Eileen R. Tabios
Saint Helena, California, the indigenous land of the Wappo
April 23, 2019

*More information about "MURDER DEATH RESURRECTION" is available on Eileen R. Tabios' website at https://eileenrtabios.com/projects/the-mdr-poetry-generator/ Information about the official MDR monograph—used by Leny to write her memoir—is available at *MURDER DEATH RESURRECTION: A Poetry Monograph* (Dos Madres Press, Loveland, OH, 2018) or https://eileenrtabios.com/poetry/murder-death-resurrection/

Introduction

Journaling with MDR Poetry

A gift of a Journal. A Poem with over a thousand lines. A gift published as a book: *MURDER DEATH RESURRECTION* by Eileen R. Tabios.

Eileen's promise: *You can randomly choose however many lines and put them together to form a new poem. And if the poet is successful, the new poem will be beautiful!*

In my other journal, I did just this and I was surprised that this promise is true. I wrote about it on *MEDIUM*, and replicate it in Appendix I. Then I decided to begin a new journal to write a one-page entry every day in response to a randomly chosen poetic line and do a free-write following what feelings, images, memories, stories the words evoke.

For three months, before going to bed, I made a date with Poetry.

The result is this book: ***Glimpses: A Poetic Memoir (through the MDR Generator)***

You should know that I recently retired after more than two decades of teaching Ethnic Studies at a state university in California. After several published books, journal articles, edited anthologies, and chapter contributions to other people's books, I declared myself free from the obligatory academic language, citations, and footnotes and such.

I wasn't going to write anymore. (In any case, who reads for length these days?)

But when Poetry calls, I listen and pay attention.

I invite you, dear reader, to see what this poetic entanglement has evoked for me… that, hopefully, evokes something Beautiful for you as well.

—Leny Mendoza Strobel
Santa Rosa, CA
A Settler on Pomo and Coast Miwok Lands

3.2.18

237 I forgot once longing for an intermission. But love is also a source of difficulty.

Is this why my life has been marked by difficulty? Because the source—Love—wills it? Love and Suffering—if we allow both to be our abiding friends—all our longings for intermissions will eventually find their angle of repose.

I took the long road to get to the point of repose. Now I long to tell the stories of how I got here. The intermissions were many—historical, political, economic, familial, personal—including some not by my choice, doing, or intention. I was merely swept along by the waves.

At breakfast today I talked about the sweep of history and the failure of neoliberalism that has its roots in Enlightenment values that were conceived by a culture of European propertied men for themselves as a form of social contract.

The contract failed as these values encountered "Others" during the age of imperial and colonial adventurism and Race was invented to justify these racial projects.

That is how I came into this world. This is the story that I know. This is the story that swept me away.

I have been looking for a different story to tell ever since. I've been looking for a story about Love.

But first I must deal with the difficulty and all the intermissions that wouldn't satiate my longings for a long time.

3.3.18

841 *I forgot darkness was the key, not the lock.*

In hindsight, the darkness that came to symbolize so many moments in my life as a Filipina—the childhood trauma of sexual abuse; the elopement at 17; the break down of a teen marriage; the disappointment and shame I brought home to my mother who had hoped there would no repeat of her children bringing home white men while the neighbors raised their eyebrows in mocking condescension; the hiding of trysts with lovers—were all keys that unlocked bits and pieces of that inner life searching for liberation. Only to find and finally be able to name the shame and guilt that isn't only personal but historical and civilizational.

Only our understanding of the dark side of history can unlock and liberate the insecure and fearful child.

The story is cruel, you see. We have all been conned by a story because it was afraid of the Dark.

The fear of Dark as Other
To be banished
To be excised
To be denied
To be untold

Is also named
Woman
Filipina
Brown Monkey
Servant of Globalization
Prostitute
Comfort Woman
Imeldific

3.4.18

413 *I forgot weeping over the language shared by a toddler and a stuffed animal*

I didn't play with stuffed animals as a toddler. It's possible I have forgotten about the dolls or stuffed animals inherited from a box sent from Philly by a Ms. Rose B. Mann, my mother's penpal. But if she had sent us dolls I am sure I didn't develop a fondness for them or I would have remembered if I did.

But I do remember the games we played outside as kids—digging holes in the dirt so that we could build a makeshift stove burner. Dig a hole, pile paper and twigs, build a fire. We had toy clay pots and sometimes we cooked rice in them.

Although, sometimes we dug holes and water would seep in, spoiling our fun. But during monsoon season it is what happens.

We played tag, hide and seek, *patintero* under the moonlight before we were called in for supper.

We ran around a lot, chasing each other, running across barriers, running away with the handkerchief, climbing trees.

I don't remember boredom
I don't remember being entertained
I don't remember and never heard the words "lacking"

We played and laughed a lot.

Today, a German writer, Andreas Weber, calls these: Erotic encounters with the biosphere and geosphere.

3.5.18

65 I forgot the grandmother who always grinned at me, unashamed her gums held no teeth.

My Apu Sinang didn't wear dentures. Nor did the other older people in our barrio back in the day. There was no shame in being toothless. And when she flashed a big smile, her cheeks would cave in, her lips against her gum straight and slightly upturned corners—she is beaming; her inner joy showing through.

I blame the purveyors of ideas of hygiene, health, and beauty for our eventual disdain for toothlessness.

Dentists started making money on dentures that were sometimes too big for the mouth. Or dentures that were clunky and ill-fitting. My Dad put up with loose dentures and he wouldn't go to the dentist because he preferred to save his money.

When we were young, instead of getting an education about keeping teeth and bones healthy, instead of being taught not to eat too many candies to avoid cavities, instead of being taught to floss everyday—we were often rushed to the dentist who was only too happy to pull out a tooth or two. Never heard of root canals, putting a cap on a cracked tooth, or a crown.

Nowadays there's tooth whitening, braces to straighten the teeth, night guard to protect from teeth-grinding.

Once the dentist recommended that at my age of 63, I can now afford to make my teeth white and straight.

I laughed aloud remembering my toothless grinning grandmother!

3.6.18

314 I forgot the zoo with retired cages

They once put my people in a zoo. It was called the 1906 St. Louis World's Fair. They brought 3,000 individuals from various tribes in the Philippines and put them in an enclosed pen and made them perform rituals and dances to entertain the white fair goers. They had to show how they killed their dogs and cook and eat them. They showed the men jousting and showing off their brutal strength. They dressed some of them in American suit and tie to show off the civilized version and then had them take photographs with the goers. Just like a selfie today.

After the zoo closed and cages were opened, some of the tribes were taken to other traveling fairs. It was still ok to show off bizarre and strange creatures then. Some went home.

In Marlon Roldan's *Bontoc Eulogy*, he created a story where one of the men supposedly fell off the ferris wheel and died and his body was never recovered. He imagined it being taken to a museum to be dissected and studied. It could be true, you know.

But we forgot about the Native American William Jones who became an anthropologist and came to work for the Chicago Field Museum and then assigned to do field work in the Philippines. He encountered the headhunting tribes. He didn't go as an Indian; he came off as an imperial emissary of anthropology (this was before Renato Rosaldo turned the discipline on its head) and his imperial ways weren't received well by the natives so they took his head.

Why do I remember these stories now? The world itself feels like a zoo now. Cages are far from being retired.

3.7.18

911 *I forgot that, under his left eye, there lurked a scar people did not acknowledge but always culled from memory.*

I do not know or remember anyone with a scar under the left eye. But I remember someone scarred by a 4th grade incident. The boy had an upset stomach and soiled his pants and released a bomb the entire classroom could smell. The teacher made everyone stand up. But this boy didn't. The teacher sent him home, his head bowed. But no one talked about that incident again to spare the boy's feelings. We were kind, you see.

But I remember that incident and have carried it around with me with a secret smile. I liked the boy but I admit this to no one...like an unacknowledged scar.

The boy and I were in the same homeroom until the end of high school. We were always paired off and teased. Maybe this is why we never spoke; never became friends until much later—much, much later—when I was already married and divorced and he was about to marry.

His kindness, intelligence, mild manners, humility, quiet spirit—I liked these about him. And he loved his county—loved it so much he never dreamed of leaving. Unlike me. I left in 1983.

The 4th grade incident was a secret I kept except on the rare occasion when classmates from primary school would get together and gossip. Haha.

The boy and the girl made another memory when during the senior prom they were again paired off: he as the consort of Miss Senior. They danced but didn't speak. At all.

Memory speaks now.

3.8.18

1,022 *I forgot how to feel the Milky Way expand simply because, upon my waist, you placed your palm.*

I've often wondered about the meditating types who could see the universe simply by closing their eyes and concentrating deeply on the breath and the third eye. They report seeing a point of light surrounded by flashes of color—blues, reds, yellows, greens, purple. They say they feel energy flow up and down the spine. Sometimes they report that what they see with eyes closed in deep meditation is the same as what astronomers describe when they point their telescopes at the sky.

Scientists also say that we are made of stars and stardust. Literally. So I've been learning to tune in more closely to this scientific fact that heretofore was only the subject of philosophy and esoteric discourse.

I long to feel a hand upon my waist and know that it is the universe that is embracing me.

In the Taoist healing system, I learn that we are energy and consciousness. The energy of the heaven, earth, sun, thunder, wind, water, mountain, and lake—is all in my breath that enters the bai hui at the top of my head and the bubbling well at the sole of my feet and collects in the dantian, my belly.

This is also the universe breathing.

3.9.18

159 *I forgot how pronouns confused me. I forgot the "she" evolving into an "I" and then back again, flustered before your gaze.*

I immediately thought of the tyranny of the English language as this gaze that disciplines. In my indigenous tongue, gender is neutral. He or she translates to Siya or Sila (they/them). Imagine how confusing it is to constantly interchange he/she/they especially in today's mandate to make sure we know people's preferred pronouns.

It is hard for me to talk about "I" so I never know what to say when I am asked: What do you do? Who are you? I don't have a problem writing about my ideas, talking story, and meditating but in a circle where we may be asked to state credentials, I get timid. Is it because I get flustered by this Gaze?

I do not have an "I" without You. Whatever it is that I have done to fill up a 25-page academic resume is just an obligation to institutional bureaucracy.

What is this reticence? Is it really oppositional and, therefore, liberating or is it a deeply felt sense of mimicry, or what academics call imposter syndrome?

I'm in a place now where I can own up to these contradictions without shame and guilt. In fact, I confess to a sense of humble knowing that I stand outside of most fences.

This liminal space has been a creative space. It has nursed many heartaches and dreams.

What is Love without suffering?

3.10.18

1,032 *I forgot Auguste Rodin drawing women while they took "melancholy pleasure" in front of him.*

The only thing I know about Rodin is his sculpture of a thinking man sitting, as if, on a toilet seat. There's one at Stanford University—don't know if it's original or not.

I haven't seen any of his drawings of women posing for him. Who is melancholy? Whose pleasure? I suppose it matters to art lovers to ponder such questions.

But I do not.

Once, I asked a friend who was taking a course on "Art History of the World" if the course included art from the non-Western world. He said, no, it didn't. How then can it be called "of the world?" Hhmpf!

I used to feel embarrassed by my lack of sophistication about the classical arts—whether of music, visual arts, opera, theatre. Even though I grew up with a mother who was a classical pianist, a grandfather who was a violinist. Even though I could recognize a Mozart melody from a Rachmaninoff—this familiarity was like a smokescreen or a veil that kept us separate from the sensuousness of animist preoccupations of barrio folks.

Rodin reminded me of this. But I no longer feel ashamed. I may not be sophisticated in the way that a Rodin gaze may imply but I know other things that are not melancholy pleasures.

3.11.18

351 *I forgot to be an angel is to be alone in a smudged gown, fingers poking through holes burnt by epistemology.*

Epistemology. How do you know what you know? How do I know that epistemology can be violent? As in "psychic and epistemic violence" of colonialism.

The first time I wore a gown was at my senior prom in high school in the Philippines. We were the first cohort given permission to hold a prom—maybe to be taken as a sign of being properly inducted into American popular culture. It was 1968 and the hippies were flowering in San Francisco.

Since the graduating class voted me as their Miss Senior, my mother made me a long chiffon gown with bling around the haltered neckline exposing bare shoulders. She even sent me to the beauty parlor where my hair was coiffed and decorated with dainty pink silk flowers. I remember not being too happy that day as the gown was just a tad short and my feet ached from ill-fitting, borrowed three-inch heels. I was nervous and giddy as we were paraded in the school's courtyard in blistering sun.

Smudged gown. Alone. Fingers poking thru holes burnt by epistemology. Strange associations, memories that must mean something. M-e-a-n-i-n-g = what does it mean that I have longed to know whether the boy who escorted me at the prom held tender feelings for me then? A longing burning holes in my dream life for decades: Why won't you love me?

A koan's meaning takes forever to show up. It turns out that this longing harkens to loving a Homeland that doesn't love me back. It turns out that the epistemic violence of being unloved is to be Alone.

3.12.18

434 I forgot, over a hill, there waited a choir.

We Filipinos are famous for our musicality. Everyone can sing. Everyone (almost) owns a karaoke mike and can belt out Original Pilipino Music (OPM) or tunes from the old days of the Bee Gees, Carole King, Frank Sinatra, or Celine Dion.

Our choirs like the Madrigal Singers or the UP Concert Chorus have won international choral competitions in Europe and Asia.

Still I was surprised that there was a Filipino choir at the top of Montsegur hill that summer day in the South of France. The choir was a small group and I can't remember now what song they were singing but my heart jumped as I heard angel voices coming from somewhere as we were walking the grounds of this ancient church where a massacre of Christian believers had occurred hundreds of years earlier during the Inquisition.

Perhaps they were drawn to sing to the ghosts of that place. To send them peace. To cleanse the Land where blood was spilled. Or perhaps they were just too moved by the beauty of the place that all they could do was to sing in response.

This happens to me quite often, too. I hum when my heart has no words to offer to the sublime moment.

There is a choir always over the hill, singing....

3.13.18

832 I forgot a flock of starlings shattering the sky's clean plate like grains of black pepper.

On Petaluma Hill Road, 30 years ago, I would often get startled by the murmuration of starlings. If I wasn't always driving or riding in a car, I would probably be drawn to my holy *tunganga*—gaze—but alas, 30 years ago I was young, restless, in a hurry, ambitious. Petaluma Hill Road goes to Sonoma State University which would become a second home to me.

I wasn't curious then about the starlings, the cow pastures along the road that gives the County its distinctive aroma, the vineyard, the hawks and vultures silently watching for prey on top of posts, or the crows and pigeons that made their perch on the corner of 4th and Farmers Lane.

I buried my head in books, learned about postcolonial criticism, decolonization, empire, colonialism. Words fed my hunger for explanations. But it was also the words that starved my heart and spirit.

But almost everyday on the way to the university on Petaluma Hill Road, the starlings were a beacon to a longing that awakened a sense of awe and wonder and curiosity.

Over the years they slowly disappeared. As with the blue jays, the hummingbirds, bees, butterflies—I started to notice the absence.

Why haven't I taken seriously my connection to these beings who dwell in this place with me?

It took a long time to come to terms with my own uprooting and disappearance from my homeland. It took a long time to be claimed by the starlings on Petaluma Hill road.

The vast Sky also longs—

3.14.18

1,088 *I forgot the opposite of fog.*

I never can get used to the sight of fog so thick that you can't see a few feet ahead of you. Once, when I was younger and still recovering from a traumatic car accident that left me unable to drive on freeways to this day, I often would commute from San Francisco and Berkeley for night classes at CAL and University of San Francisco and then drive home in thick fog…slowly…very slowly.

I didn't notice fog in the islands' lowlands. I suppose up the Cordillera mountains in the north they experience fog. Nothing unusual.

Fog—what is the science of it? How is it different from low clouds hanging over the hills on certain days of winter or spring?

My mother, in one of her journal entries, writes about the mystical experience she felt while flying thru clouds on her first airplane ride to the U.S. She said it felt like heaven or close to it.

I, on the other hand, feel only nervousness when flying through clouds at 33,000 ft. Thank goodness for instruments that tell directions.

These last few days, mornings are foggy. The white blanket over the hills and the dew drops on the leaves of the budding honeysuckle remind me that Spring is near.

Although climate change is altering the cycles that have been fairly stable for thousands of years, there are more and more alarms about the rapid melting of the ice on the polar caps, the receding glaciers in the Himalayas. We've been warned that fresh water scarcity is going to cause droughts leading to crop failure, hunger….

What is the opposite of fog? I do not really know.

3.15.18

1,145 I forgot a poem with a certain flickering light—not bright, fragile, but one senses its dependability for never dying into dark!

Today I received a reply from Linda Hogan, poet/novelist whom I've admired for so long. I remember the year when I read all of her books—*Power, Rounding out Human Corners, Woman Who Watches Over the World, Solar Storm*—she is the one who lured me into indigenous literature with her story of healing trauma and the power of love, indigenous love.

She is that light, you see, that fragility, not bright—and yet the dark never conquers the worst of our nature, our follies, weaknesses—ruined by genocidal wars, alcohol, depression, etc.

She loves horses and other animals as teachers, as healers.

I'm not anywhere near as good as a writer as she is. I'm not a writer I don't think. I am honest, that I know. And I have plenty of time to think, meditate, question, wonder.

That's what I hope my life has been so far—a poem with a flickering light. Not bright, fragile—but dependable and will never die in the dark.

I want Noah, my only grandson, to remember me that way. Or maybe he will remember differently. That's the nature of a flicker, I suppose. A reminder not to hold on too tightly to expectations no matter how noble-sounding.

Maybe in the 4th and 5th dimensions such desires do not matter much.

3.16.18

469 *I forgot the audacity of cruelty.*

"But Brother Stu, why are your people so cruel?" asked the Teduray friend of Stu Schlegel when he was trying to explain the discrimination suffered by gay folks in the U.S.

If I were to judge American culture given the violence of guns, shootings in our schools, have I violated the yoga sutra of non-judgment?

The *yamas* and *niyamas* that anyone on the yoga path must cultivate does not include judging others. Krishnamurti says regarding violence: we can study it, reflect on it, but we do not judge because we may not know the whole truth or story behind someone's cruelty. How they got that way. What contributed to their violence?

Well, we do know. We can discern root causes: disconnection and isolation, loneliness, fear, shame, anger—all the things that separate a person from their divinity and goodness which is their true Self.

So by the time cruelty becomes audacious there's already a culture that made that possible.

How have I experienced cruelty? It's hard to answer this question now because I have worked for many decades to heal from the cruelty of colonial mentality and racism. If racial micro-aggressions are a form of cruelty then, yes, I still suffer them but I also know that whatever is projected onto me is not me. But if the cruel one is to be helped in seeing himself as cruel and cringes at what he has become—would they automatically change? Does their world view offer that possibility?

3.19.18

692 I forgot him singing a shivering woman with no defense as soldiers arrive to do what they did to her and her too-young daughters.

There stood a silent witness to the horrors done to women.

I've just returned from a weekend retreat with indigenous women elders and young indigenous women that was quickly summoned in the light of a #metoo moment within the local native community.

In the circle, one after another, twenty five women said:
I was molested
I was raped
I was abused
I was betrayed

By men in the community.
Men who are leaders
Men who are protected by other women
Men who are damaged

Tears flowed.

In the end soothed by the words of a wise elder.

The perpetrators have done things to your body.
But they took nothing from you.
They didn't take the stardust in you.
Remember your strength and your Source.
Cry. Let the tears flow.
That is how we become human.

But you are warriors.
You will rise up.
You will end this scourge in your life.
We will heal our communities.

3.20.18

340 *I forgot Microsoft snooping on our passions.*

Microsoft, Facebook, Google, Instagram, Pinterest, Snapchat, Amazon—they are all snooping on our passions.

Sometimes I click on an ad just to tease their algorithms. I never buy what I don't need.

They will never know what my passions truly are because my passions do not sell products. I have nothing to sell or buy.

I want the gift economy to be my currency of choice. I want to invite my friends to gift each other with intangible things like: going for a walk together; home cooking and inviting friends to eat with you; hosting events.

Yes, of course, we will need money—but the challenge is to experiment with sharing our passions with each other.

Brenda's passion is wine; Karen's passion is golf; Ilaya's passion is unschooling Heru; Pinay's passion is plant medicine. My passion is books. Noemi's passion is helping others.

The challenge is to do something good, to spread good deeds. Kindness. Generosity.

It is not enough to celebrate our individual passions within a clique.

The world is big. What do I gift to the Holy in Nature?

3.22.18

259 *I forgot to savor my childhood house where grandmother gave births with abundant abandon, where generations died more radiant than a sun's implosion.*

Makes me think of Hiroshima and Nagasaki. Makes me think of the implosion of Manila in WW2 as the elephants were dancing. There were casualties but how come I never heard the stories and because I didn't hear them, the stories didn't enter my body. And so the war never ended.

A blank childhood. A stolen childhood. A damaged childhood. Saved by the memory of my Lola and of my mother—giving birth naturally. Midwife Dang Pinang—how did she learn how to be a midwife? Dang Mary, her sister—godmother of my oldest sister, she sent her money so she can go to college. Such generosity paid for our colonial dreams.

If I could undo all of these internalized narratives of the West, I would. I must.

Join the growing community of folks who are doing the same—finding a new story to tell away from Dow Jones index, economic indicators, etc. Must redefine happiness and joy. Redefine work. Redefine currency away from money.

Back to caring for one another like a village. Where I know my child is also your child. Where we do not compete for awards and prizes. Where we do not climb ladders and perch on top. Where we do not ogle at celebrities. Where we do not seek attention. Where humility is the measure of leadership and leadership is the other word for servanthood.

Until then let the Sun implode. We probably deserve our disappearance.

3.23.18

592 *I forgot rain does not truly forgive.*

This is the second poem I read today where Nature is anthromorphized to reflect our human character. We project all kinds of feelings on Rain, Water, Sun, Fire, Air, Metal, Wood.

I wonder if these projections can actually be barriers to getting to know these Beings and having a relationship with them. What does it mean? What would that look like? Can we have a relationship without humanizing other Beings.

How does Rain forget to forgive?

At least in Greg Sarris' *How a Mountain Was Made*, we hear of stories of the village where Rain goes away in sorrow and returns only when she realized that she and the village need each other.

Weather people talk about severe weather with words like "battle the weather; the weather is horrific; the weather is raging…"

As if Nature is an enemy to be vanquished, tamed, overcome.

Someday we will all be humbled.

The October Firestorm (2017) reminded us that we are not in control.

So Rain does not truly forgive. She doesn't need to. Does she even know the concept of forgiveness? Rain is. Now if you are Dine/Navajo, you know that Rain is your ancestor returning.

3.23.18

699 I forgot joining gypsies to adore Juana specifically for her madness.

I only know of one Sor Juana, a 16th century saint who was accused of being mad. But I don't know the real story. Can a Netflix drama series be trusted? Did Sor Juana really become a lover to the viceroy's wife? Or were the women in love with her fierceness, her courage to write and to be published—something that they could not have—this freedom to be?

Yesterday I was interviewed by Ilaya for KPFA's Roots Communications' International Women's Month. She asked me:

> What makes a woman whole?
> What is an empowered woman?
> Duty or Love?
> What will you do in your retirement?

Every question has an implicit assumption. And so must reveal those assumptions. Whose are they? What do the assumptions say about the culture we live in? Can this culture change seeing how damaging it has been to the Earth? Can we unravel these assumptions and rewrite or reframe our stories?

Like this line about gypsies adoring Juana for her madness? What or who are the gypsies? Oh, we know the stereotypes we have about them as displaced peoples. Hmmm. I do not really know what a gypsy is. Or what madness is.

Juana was mad to a world that couldn't bear an empowered woman!

3.24.18

106 *I forgot Mom beginning to age when she started looking at the world through heartbreaking resignation.*

Aging is not a pathology unless one belongs to a culture that defies age. I have never claimed belonging to this culture. Even though that may be a considered a contradiction. For how can we not belong in a culture where you have become the self you are now that is capable of denying that belonging?

Perhaps that is what is heartbreaking—the privilege of living in a bubble where one can still claim a sense of detachment from the very thing one is already entangled with.

Still, we must not feel resigned to the way things are because we are constantly in motion. As I am aging I pray that I may continue to deepen this erotic encounter with the world. To continue to learn what makes all encounters poetic.

Today, five year old Alethea said "it's not about winning and losing—it's just about learning how to hop on one foot" as we played hopscotch on the sidewalk.

Bayo and EJ arrived today from India with daughter Alethea and son Kyah. The event at the Unitarian Church was well attended considering all other choices people had on the same night: Greg Sarris, Don Miguel Ruiz, and Shomrei Torah.

3.25.18

179 I forgot you falling asleep in my skin to dream.

I still sometimes think of a Koan that has been in my dream for decades. Unable, seemingly, to unravel its mystery completely—therein lies the ongoing energetic load of the question.

Does a dream carry energy to the object of the dream? This seems contrary to the Jungian premise that all the images in a dream represent parts of the dreamer's self.

Certainly within the dreamer there's always a Koan—that mystery that we're always trying to hold on to. Wishing to release it and wishing or imagining it to be vanished from memory. Either way is unknown.

To fall asleep. To dream. A Someone, a Koan. Can be a mere idea, memory. Energy.

In other dimensions, third or fourth, who knows?

If I were more attached or sensitive to those realms, I might get an inkling.

3.28.18

966 *I forgot.*

But then I saw his name on FB and I decided to send him a message:

"Hi, my name is Elenita Mendoza. Do you remember me?"
"Of course! I am one of your many admirers…"

Fifty years ago, this boy tormented me. He and his friends called themselves Vostoks and they cat-called and followed me around the high school campus. Those days he made it known that he had a crush on me.

Today he's married with four kids. I remember that I didn't like him because he wasn't too good looking, not too smart (I was arrogant then!)—but he's just a boy whose name I remembered. He may have even courted me but I snubbed him.

Anyway, these high school reunion stories remain in the present as a diffracted, entangled story of a young girl's life confused by philosophical questions that I couldn't fathom or articulate at that age.

Well then, why do I get frustrated with freshmen in my classes who do not yet have formed opinions of what they believe about who they are?

Mercy. I wonder what they'll do with Gloria Anzaldua and Sherman Alexie for their midterms?

3.28.18

856 *I forgot a girl singing, "I will become Babaylan! With notes only virgin boys can muster, only dogs can hear!*

Oh dear, I don't want to utter the word Babaylan these days. It's loaded with my hurt feelings towards someone. Let her have the word and let her carry the work forward.

I have never desired to become a Babaylan. While I have resurrected the history with very little knowledge to show for it really I was looking for something to connect with a heritage that is powerful, that is specific.

At that time, it was empowering and it was necessary to create discourse and practice around it—thus, the Center for Babaylan Studies.

After a while, as experience and perception evolve, other things come into view and shift us away from what had given us a mooring. We let go. We move on. We meet other folks. We ask new questions.

We look deep as quantum physics always asks of us; we look to the past of our ancestors and bring their stories forward; we touch other beings and be in communion.

This ever-enlarging circle of relationships and entanglements has a refrain: Be Here, Be Home.

Spring is here. The pear tree is blooming. The fuji apple is coming along; and I don't think we'll have apricots this year.

3.28.18

224 I forgot commitment costs.

Was that a commitment we made to each other? To never speak to each other again and to never speak of what went on between us to anyone? We will always have these memories, you said. They are sacred so we will not squander them to gossip.

So I have remained silent but oh how tempting to spill secrets to burst the bubbles of shallow friendships and polite company.

Ginny, the other one you loved, has already disappeared. I made up a story about this, too. She knew so she must be angry that what she believed was her story was a lie after all. She never liked me. I think she knows.

But this is all storymaking. A projection of my mind which has nothing to do with Real.

Still we are already entangled whether we like it or not. Whether we acknowledge it or not.

That's why I like Lani Misalucha's "Bukas na Lang Kita Mamahalin". Someday when we might find ourselves unafraid.

3.29.18

59 I forgot the grandfather who willingly faced a fire, fist trembling at the indifferent sky.

I still don't know if the rumor is true but I like the story that has claimed me: the Luna brothers—Antonio and Juan—are the siblings of my great grandfather, Joaquin.

Antonio—the military general who was anti-imperialist and fought for the independence of the Philippines and he was assassinated by Aguinaldo who capitulated to the Americans. There's a movie about him: "Heneral Luna."

Juan—the national artist known best for Spoliarium. Trained in European style painting of the time, he won many awards. He was also a known womanizer along with Jose Rizal and Antonio. They were all illustrados. In a fit of jealousy Juan murdered his wife and mother-in-law but was acquitted on account of insanity. He was deported to Hong Kong and lived in exile.

Joaquin was the governor of La Union (now named Luna, La Union after him). He worked for the tobacco monopoly, he was a violinist and he was sent to the 1904 St. Louis World Fair to represent the government. Supposedly he had two families. I don't know which family we are, most likely the illegitimate one.

How did these Luna brothers become infamous? How did they become illustrados and how did their descendants squander their legacy of greatness?

I do not know. I know the stories are alive and need to be told.

I am still shaking my fist at them—only the Sky who is not indifferent stands as a witness to the silent response.

3.30.18

332 I forgot life defined through the credit card.

Today I had to order new checks from the bank. I wanted to ask the teller if I'm the last of the dinosaurs who wouldn't do online banking but I didn't. Why should I give him the pleasure of mockery?

I do not know anything about cryptocurrencies either.

Let the world leave me behind. I feel the narrowing of my materialistic horizon. I prefer it this way.

And I suppose Pankaj Mishra would agree that this mimicry of neoliberal promises must end not by policies or law but by individuals choosing to opt out of a dream.

Of course, the wars will never end because it keeps the economy going. They have to keep manufacturing and selling weapons to Iraq, Saudi Arabia, Syria, Yemen, Iran, and everywhere else.

Also sell guns to hunters of animals and even allowing the import of trophy animals. They just introduced kangaroos in Wyoming for future hunters.

The world of credit cards and debts keep all the worker bees too busy to stop and think.

Bayo Akomolafe is on to something here: indigenous wisdom + quantum theory + agential materialism.

Ethnoautobiography as portal.

Shamanic practices—

Invites all to slow down and be lost.

3.31.18

673 I forgot stepping into a story I falsely thought belonged to me.

And now I know that the story that flowed out of the 17th and 18th century Enlightenment and Age of Reason—rise of individualism, private property, self-interest, democracy, freedom—all these philosophies that became globalized and universalized – is not mine.

You could argue, of course, that we are all conscripted by the story and there's no stepping outside of it. It was Derrick Jensen who I first heard say: Do not identify with civilization. To wean ourselves from this story is to not identify with it.

Yes, you still have to be part of the capitalist system as a necessity. You still need to buy industrial food, you still need to pay rent or mortgage.

But do not be claimed or owned by it.

I told Cal today that I do not identify with the U.S., with its sports culture, with Stephen King's novels, with the cult of individualism.

It perhaps still rattles him a bit but it is good to be reminded or good to say aloud what it is we don't believe in anymore: neoliberalism, 'us' versus 'them', West and the Rest.

Of course, spiritual bypassing remains an option. Don't take it.

4.1.18

605 *I forgot my father is not Idi Amin of Uganda.*

And as notorious as Idi Amin was, isn't he a product of history and a narrative of dispossession and later what Pankaj Mishra calls appropriative mimicry? Mimetic desire gone awry when colonized countries realized they could no longer tolerate the boot of empire.

Dictators rise to take advantage of a people looking for a compass to show them a way out of humiliation, anger. In the process of eliminating their enemies, they also diminish their own humanity… then sliding into a tighter hold on power as they must know their reigns do not last forever.

Aren't all patriarchs dictators in their small domains? This is how they are socialized to take care of women and children. The division of labor in a relationship was also loaded with values and worth under an economic arrangement.

As my father chose to sell bibles for his main income, my mother taught piano to augment his meager salary. We raised pigs and chickens to feed ourselves.

Dad was wise and frugal. Mom was, too. In the simplicity of our material possessions we were rich in community and sharing and nurturing of one another.

But we were also taught to desire more: education, marriage to white partners, careers…

No wonder letting go of the story is painful.

Where to find our Wildness again?

4.2.18

14 *I forgot our hair had whitened...*

And we have become crones. Wise women, gracious women. Women who do not dye their hair to look young. Women who do not put toxic chemicals on their hair, on their nails, on their face, on their bodies.

So many ways of seducing them into thinking they compete with younger women.

Afraid of loss. Of death. Of disappearance from the gaze of adoring men.

My hair has whitened. My age spots are showing, wrinkles line my eyes. My skin under my arms is sagging and wrinkling (oh, I love the sound of this word!).

But all of these signs speak of years of stashing away memories of good times, sad times, joyful, mournful, ecstatic times. Times with lovers. Loving many and often. Of love songs crooned in the shower or while driving alone in car. Karaoke to old tunes pining for the one who got away.

We smile. Our hair has whitened. We have loved well. Lived poetically.

We planted seeds. We harvested herbs and made white sage bundles, oregano pesto, bok choy and chard casserole, dried apples and pears. We made bouquets of flowers. We gave away to neighbors.

Our hair has whitened.

We lived well.

4.3.18

483 I forgot when memory became a colander with generous holes.

And perhaps we need those big-holed colanders as sieve for unwanted memories of a broken past. But wait. Why call the past 'broken'? What is my frame of reference here? Sure the past reeks of colonial imperialist ventures that trampled islands and archipelagos. But we are still here. We have not been made to disappear. Perhaps disfigured a bit—our sense of self not quite recovered from shadows swallowed from the persuasion of white love, from the force of ideology stamped with divine signatures.

Everything can be reframed. Stories can be edited. Memory as the drama of the mind.

The mystery of consciousness.

Perhaps it is the Wild that has escaped the holes of the colander.

I've been pondering this for a while now. I think of Tongva elder, L Frank, saying: They've taken nothing from us. We are still stardust. Remember your strength. Remember your Source.

How do we tell this to each other?

4.4.18

469 I forgot the audacity of cruelty.

Yesterday was "Punish a Muslim" day; supposedly it was started in England. Not sure who's behind it but the ugly flyer was offering points for cruel acts committed against Muslims from the throwing acid on a face to bombing the Haj for 2,000 points.

Whoever started this prank demonstrates the audacity of cruelty. But there's also a certain toopidity that makes it so.

Reminds me of trolls that I see on FB, mostly those defending Duterte's drug war and other acts.

Sometimes it's easy to dismiss the lack of sophistication of such moves. Pedestrian, mediocre, naïve—whatever else may be attached to such acts come from a perch of privilege. A mockery. A derogatory attitude towards folks with less education.

But isn't this what we are trying to get away from—language that divides, alienates, us versus them?

4.5.18

1,146 *I forgot the present is thin, and the past thick.*

Especially when you get past 50 and from then on you know that your past will always be thicker than your present.

I remember my Dad always wanting to tell stories about his remote past—about people and times I didn't know or care about. I should have known better that I will regret not letting him remember. I would regret not remembering my father's history.

I want to blame something, some peoples for this—the incursion of ideas that were imposed on us. This Protestant evangelical version that erased a lot of things that I have been harping about since then for decades now. It's no longer enough to lament.

It's important to reclaim those lessons; to re-story my life. In a world that is moving fast, not good not to have solid footing.

Noah needs to know what to put his faith and trust in.
Maybe he'll learn it from the garden.
Maybe he'll learn it from his father's devotion or his mother's garden.

Maybe there will be that one teacher that lights a fire in his belly.

To discover the power of language and imagination.
To understand the power of history and our power to rewrite it.

May the Earth speak...
My prayers touching his skin as they ride an energy and wave of light...
From here to Fairfax.

4.6.18

731 *I forgot the chill of kissing the wrong man.* O lifetime of pearls!

In my culture, we do/did Ungngo—the exchange of life-giving Breath. What seems like a sniffing away as one presses their cheek to you—is their way of saying "I exchange the breath of life with you."

How much more profound is this than kissing? What is the origin of kissing?

I may wish for kisses now to be more like kisses of affection, fondness, kinship, not romantic.

Although I do remember when I kissed someone ever so lightly on the lips. Shyly. And I remember when a woman artist tried to kiss me and I pulled back confused by her sudden approach. I didn't know what it meant. I think she was very lonely even though she was very famous. She had just been recognized as a Mobil Art awardee for her huge woven tapestries.

The mystery of a kiss visited upon lovers who didn't plan on falling for each other.

The mystery of a kiss that unravels all the ribbons wound around a heart made of rules and policed manners.

The mystery of a kiss that breaks protocol. I will and cannot own you even if I wish it so. But at least we made memories to last a lifetime.

4.7.18

124 *I forgot aching for fiction that would not chasten my days.*

Browsing through movies on Netflix is no fun as they are always about white folks—their history, their loves, their royalties, their adventures, their endless search for more —whatever the 'more' is.

Same with the literature fiction section at Copperfields Books.

At least there's Bollywood movies. Today, I watched *Love Per Square Feet* about the ambition of young corporate workers to own real estate property—usually or in this movie—a 500 sq ft. apartment in a high rise.

A man and woman scheme to apply in a lottery for one of these government-funded Lotto to combine their incomes and be able to afford ownership. Both of them are in relationships with others but they eventually realize that they are falling in love. You can imagine the rest.

I wonder what these ambitions would look like when Noah comes of age. What would be important for him? How will he make his choices? How would he weigh his father's and mother's values? How would he make his own?

What are the useful fictions that do not rest on Whiteness and all its aberrant forms?

Neoliberalism and capitalism will fail eventually as natural resources are poisoned and depleted.

What would humans look like?

4.8.18

104 *I forgot jasmine insisted it was the scent of gold.*

Yes, it is gold. Literally. The honeysuckle is gold. Jasmine, sampaguita, daphne. I do not know how to describe the fragrance—a bit of citrus, a bit of honey, a hint of lilac. No, not really.

So far science hasn't been able to create an app where you can smell the scent of jasmine when you tap a picture of it.

Distill, extract it and put it in lotions, perfume, soaps, air freshener, incense. Maybe make a synthetic chemical version.

For me it's the 30-year-old vine climbing up to the second-floor deck blooming in the spring and the bees happily sipping nectar.

For me it's my Apu's vine, my connection to my roots, to magical women who made garlands of jasmine picked in the early morning before the buds open.

4.9.18

346 *I forgot gifts carefully differentiated among recipients—the matron's painstaking definitions of servants versus those served.*

Today I was invited to the opening exhibit of Joan Baez's paintings of Mischief Makers—the civil rights leaders of the 60s and 70s who changed the world while making mischief.

The invitation came from Greg Sarris to be on his guest list. When the tickets arrived I noticed that the tickets were $250 per person. I gasped. I wouldn't pay for these tickets on my own no matter how badly I wanted to meet Joan Baez.

I become conscious of class hierarchies in such affairs. This one specially is to benefit the Social Justice Center at Sonoma State University.

What is even the status of social justice on this campus?

Just in the prior week, my students of color walked out in frustration. White students defending their whiteness refused to listen. What is transformative education but the dismantling of systems that perpetuate the silencing and negating of experiences outside of the white norm?

Who are the servants? Who is serving? How do we dismantle this binary?

Redefine servants as leaders.
Redefine leaders as social justice advocates.
Disentangle from fame and fortune.

4.10.18

1,028 *I forgot how to perceive with tenderness.*

Aw shucks! This is a painful reminder. This 'tenderness' thing is not my strong suit. Like—how do you make your way in this culture with 'tenderness'?

And besides, I've had a tough life—rebel, impulsive, confused, probably should have been diagnosed as postcolonial trauma instead of internalized shame and then the only way to fight back is by being tough-minded, logical, rational.

Well, all these lessons have been learned now. Surely I can practice tenderness now—nothing to lose. My heart is open.

But Dang! Some of my groups on FB just bore me and irritate me and I don't feel any tenderness for these folks.

Except for B. I even sense his energy in these photos. He is trying not to be visible. I have all kinds of stories in my head about him to entertain myself. Lol.

He's appeared twice in my dreams lately—all smiles and loving—so that is nice.

Let me be tender towards these moments and memories.

Let me be tender towards the young girl who is pretty and well admired by boys but who didn't know what to do with youthful flirtations.

Let me be tender towards the academic woman—admired and respected by many.

Let me be tender towards Cal who deserves it the most.

Let me tender towards the years to come…

4.12.18

756 I forgot I composed this song that would turn you into ice, so you will know with my next note what it means to shatter into tiny pieces the universe will ignore.

It is not so bad that someday all we hoped to be remembered by will be ignored. But there is always a remainder. No matter how we try to rub out something, there will be pieces that will remind me...

Of the difficult mother in law
Of the molesters of my innocence
Of the ghosts that showed up but weren't fed so may still be hungry
Of the lover who is not spoken of ever

The universe writes the song, not I. I am being sung. We are being sung. Nothing is ignored. Nothing is forgotten.

I wish I had more certainty about the things I know intuitively, e.g. that energy travels following our thoughts and intentions. Like the moon tugging at the tides. Like the tugging of the moon in the tides of our bodies.

Such attunement to the rhythms of nature, such sensitivity to her breathing is what makes us feel alive. Vitality. Joy. Tenderness.

It's all music.

4.12.18

481 *I forgot no alley exists without flavor.*

Alleys are dark and narrow and sometimes a shortcut thru a neighborhood of nipa huts…perhaps squatters or settlers from rural areas crowding in the city's alleys where children play in the streets: hide and seek, tumbang preso, frog's leap, and other games of a childhood long ago.

In our alley we played with small clay pots and we can actually cook rice in them. They came in sets including the stove where we used matchsticks and dry leaves for fuel.

When the rice is cooked we picked the leaves of a plant that is shaped like a salad bowl to use as plate. The alleys of childhood is where I spent most of our playtime…until it got dark.

I will never forget a ghost I saw when I was about 10. I can only see a form of a white shirt and shorts but couldn't see anyone and there was no answer when I asked who is there.

It could be this is one reason why I am not attracted to the idea of having actual encounters with spirit beings who may not be good. They can be mischievous or tricksterish. Could be hungry ghost.

But must learn to heal the hungry ghosts, too.

4.13.18

410 *I forgot geometry.*

How auspicious that yesterday I was chatting with high school classmates about our Geometry teacher, Mrs. Umali, who, by the way, is still alive and attended the recent 50th high school reunion.

Mrs. Umali was a good teacher but I couldn't wrap my head around angles, hypotenuse, circumference, and all other geometry-related concepts.

So I often daydreamed and stared outside and she always called me back. *Elenita, stop daydreaming!*

Oh, if only she knew then that daydreaming is a gift. I was practicing Holy Tunganga —silent contemplation…a diffused attention as in Zen's emptying out; staring at nothing but in the process quieting the mind and allowing Awareness to grow.

So I was an imaginative child given to philosophizing, brooding about the meaning of life as I picked up my older sister's red book of Mao and Victor Frankl's *Search for Meaning.*

I was a confused teen about love and attraction. I was repulsed by the attention of homely boys but I was filled with a longing to be desired by a boy I've known since second grade.

The high school reunion folks reminded me that I was the pretty, popular one but I never perceived myself in that way.

I forgot Geometry but I fell in love with psychology when I picked up F. Scott Fitzgerald's *Tender is the Night.* How strange that I now don't remember what that was about.

When mimicry is the belly of an education, forgetting is a gift.

4.14.18

62 I forgot a country somewhere, always at the opposite of where I stand on earth.

At lecture the other day, I mentioned to students that the concept of nation or country are socially constructed and therefore can be challenged and contested. The boundaries are not fixed. They are porous. Moveable. Shifting.

The Philippines—look at it now—crumbling under the weight of its borrowed institutions from the West. Subverted by a culture that refuses linearity, boxes, and "civil" discourse. This is a "country" built upon bilateral kinship systems and matriarchal lineages.

Centuries of colonization will not erase the indigenous remains no matter how Catholic folks are.

Colonial damage is real. It is wrought by the country where I am—USA—not to say that there were no conflicts in pre-colonial communities but there is evidence that when conflicts arose the indigenous sense of justice was not punitive but restorative. Both offender and offended are addressed. An assurance that everyone is taken cared of and that the offender is restored. Teduray justice.

These indigenous values are challenged as more and more Indigenous Peoples convert to Christianity, get educated, go to the city, even go abroad.

But those who are decolonizing and re-indigenizing in the diaspora are reclaiming their indigenous mind.

Coming full circle.

The country I forgot.

4.15.18

1,107 *I forgot that meditation, if conducted deeply, must harvest pain.*

Pain is a Gift. Don't let anyone tell you that it isn't. Tonight I met Joan Baez and I've been watching Youtube videos just to be familiar with her music and story as I know very little about her. Not that I know much more now but public figures like her are a mystery. We do not know the Pain of their lives but what we have is their music and paintings.

My small public life of scholarship, of phenomenological meditation on the process of decolonization and indigenization, is born of pain.

As childbirth is painful, the baby is always a gift of mystery, of love's creative impulse.

Pain, if you work on it, following Freire's naming, reflection, action is liberating to some extent.

Complete your liberation with the realization of your Self vs the mind (Vedanta).
Keep grounded in Presence.
Nurture community.
Make time for solitude and silence.

All pain is fecund.

The pain of loss of people with whom we had ecstatic relations that changed our lives.
The pain of being sovereign.
The pain of being forgotten.

But in the end such loss and pain is alchemized into a glimpse of the beauty of Transience and only Memory remains.

4.16.18

183 *I forgot water becoming like love: miserable and lovely.*

It's been raining. Hail in some places blanketing everything for a few minutes. Rain from clouds…from the condensation of water on the earth. The miracle of water as snow in the Himalayas or in the Sierra Madre mountains or the arctic ice melting. It is Love because it supports all life. Sea water protecting whales, dolphins, jellyfish, and all who live in Grandmother Ocean. River water or freshwater in lakes. We use it to irrigate farms, to quench our thirst, to bathe our skin, to cook our food.

Water—She is Love. And yet so many do not love her back. They love oil more even though they can't drink oil.

Flint, Michigan. West Virginia chemical city. Fracking chemicals end up in water from taps in fracked areas. Water poisoned by plastic that is from oil…that ends up in the trash…that ends up in the bellies of fish that we eat…that poisons our blood and cells.

What is this misery that compels us to disown what we Love? Or fail to acknowledge? Water is Life. Water is Sacred.

It is difficult to think of Water…as Life…as Love…as Sacred.

Sometimes I want to believe that our Story is that of Forgetting.

4.17.18

192 I forgot audacity, at times, must be a private affair.

I wonder if others perceive me as an Audacious one. I am guessing the majority of the answer would be Yes!—but would they know what's behind it?

I have a longing to reveal a lot more. Like Carolyn North does in *Ecstatic Relations* where she recounts love stories that can only be described as ecstatic.

So why this privacy? This covering or reticence to reveal these stories that have shaped the visible forms of my life?

Perhaps the babaylan figure and the babaylan-inspired work is merely the projection of my soul's longings for a Home that is rooted in Place. The homeland is that Place.

And yet—whereas I used to dream of lahar erasing my home from the map—today I don't dream much. There is a quiet in that realm.

Between the gift of shamanic journeying and its revelations and the quieting of the Mind thru a yoga practice and a Taoist practice—or Vedanta awareness of the self vs the mind…I do not cling too tightly.

I've been feeling grief the last few days—perhaps because the gray skies have returned, making me feel that I should be in a hibernation cave.

Honoring Grief and letting myself cry without feeling afraid that it may not pass or that the body is sick—I acknowledge this presence of stories.

I treat myself to a boba at Sunny's to cheer me up.

I go back to my quilting project…
Coaxing my audacious spirit to speak in my dream…

4.18.18

728 *I forgot the ziggurat tattooed on an inner thigh, an area where inscription must have surfaced with anguish, then desperation, then a hymn long forgotten as I'd forgotten how to attend anyone's church.*

Trigger word: tattoo. I am always asked when or if I'll ever get a batok, a hand-tapped indigenous tattoo. So many folks have been tattooed by Lane Wilcken and others as they reclaim a heritage or connection to roots.

It is a beautiful gesture: a rite of passage. A tattoo represents one's love, in this case, for a lost homeland—lost to colonialism. Or erasure—it becomes an amulet against forgetting.

"You are already tattooed in your heart," Lane once told me. I am satisfied with that observation.

I suppose if my henna temporary tattoo in '97 was permanent, I will always be reminded of the car accident that nearly killed me.

In recovery I invited a henna artist to decorate my arm as it healed a 6-inch scar on my right arm.

But this was a moment in my life that, in hindsight, now marks a kind of turning point.

And there are many turning points in my life. If I had a tattoo for each of them, I might run out of skin.

So I content myself that I am tattooed in my heart with love whose boundaries keep rippling outwards. Sometimes I can even see the disappearance of form and flesh as energy moves beyond matter.

4.18.18

1,155 I forgot the poem written because its author, "at the end of life, must stagger back towards love."

But what if life doesn't end? And Love always is. Such lines remind me of the external references of culture and language and worldview that write the Poem. That write of endings and staggerings backward as if in the interim of living something (like Love) was forgotten and life becomes mundane, stoic and stale, flat…

But it is still all Love—those moments are part of Love because Love always includes pain, inconvenience, stupor, dullness, boredom—all of which are meant to keep our desire on fire so that we may search for Unity/Union within and without. So that we may reach for a state of calm, balance, equanimity.

This is called Commitment.

Creatures of habit formed by romantic notions of patriarchy, individualism and end of life scenario of heaven and hell do not serve us well.

So perhaps it is a good sign that Trump represents the Shadow—the culture that has long misled us.

The emptiness that most folks fill with material want is speaking loudly now. The younger ones who have the eyes to see and heart to hear no longer want to play along.

This masterful but empty self gives way to a desire for community.

Kapwa, I always say under my breath. Let this enter the English language.

4.19.18

930 *I forgot true love is never chaste.*

This one is for you, Carolyn, my 80-year-old friend. Your love is democratic, you said, and you've fallen in love—deeply and sensuously—with many even while you were married. And this is the love I want, too, and I have loved in the same way but how come I can't write and talk about these loves?

I need to be liberated from this concept of chastity. Eros is not chaste. Eros loves with all of one's body, soul, heart, mind. Eros/Love transcends our puny, narrow, dangerous concept of love as a monogamous relationship inside a marriage.

Love—when it is democratic—is love for a friend with whom one has shared her heart and soul, deepest desires, longings, Love—is to be witnessed and honored and received without masks. Naked. Honest.

I know now that this is the love of R that I didn't understand then. So it scared me. Perhaps rightly so for I would have lost perspective in the madness of such attention. In the real world, this doesn't work.

So how to love without falling into the trap of ethical boundaries? When this type of love requires a maturity of understanding of purusha vs. prakriti.

No tamas.

4.20.18

1,165 *I forgot the medicinal nature of Tango.*

Or dance of any kind…as long as you become aware of your body from the soles of your feet to the crown of your head.

Carolyn asked me what music I would like to dance to. I said 'Latin' and then she told me to close my eyes.

Breathe and focus your attention on your feet. Notice your toes, your arches, the ball of your feet. Feel. Then notice your ankles, your legs, your knees, your thigh, your hip joint. Your lower back, your torso, your shoulders, your chest. Your neck. Your arms. Your fingers.

For an hour she guided me thru her voice. I hear her sing and she encourages me to make sounds but I couldn't at first as I was paying attention to my movement.

I tried not to be self-conscious. I tried to let go and flow…feeling the floor, the warmth of the sun thru the round hole on top of the yurt. The buzzing of a fly that flew in.

After an hour she led me to the bed and we were quiet and held hands briefly. I thanked her. I told her of the electric energy across my right arm—heart meridian—I like to think it's my heart expanding.

It was joyful and magical.
It wasn't Tango.
But it was Dance.
And it was Medicine.

I woke up next day feeling alive and joyful. I even cooked breakfast.

It felt like a new day.

I started thinking of coming home again…

4.21.18

955 *I forgot algebra failing to succor when relationships were inevitably destabilized by indigenous cell memory.*

What do we rely on for succor? What assuages? What comforts? Knowledge? Science? Math? Physics?—all potentially providing an objective, albeit abstract, story that promises knowing for sure. We call it getting an Education.

But what has all this educating led to? Plastic in the ocean. Nuclear waste in search of where to dump and hide. Disappearing species. Poisoned water in Flint, MI. Hunger, war refugees. Ice caps melting. And the list is endless.

I can almost hear indigenous people say: We told you so. We've been trying to tell you so. But your hearts are cold and numb and your soul has become arid. Your body numbed out by alcohol and opioids.

Where is the light that shines thru the planks of a broken roof?

She is learning to dance
Weaving
Carving a canoe
Making art
Doing embroidery
Singing
Meditating
Chanting
Walking
Sitting in silence
Praying

Murmurations rising from indigenous memory remembering what it takes to appease the gods who take care of the seeds and water and that womb that births all...

4.22.18

1,069 *I forgot infants thrown up then caught by stabbing bayonets.*

I forgot where I've read accounts of this—either Indian wars or the Philippine American war. What difference does it make—these wars are related because a lot of the U.S. soldiers deployed to the Philippines just after the Indian wars.

The cruelty and brutality of these acts do not surprise. These are banal acts as evil is banal—I think it was Hannah Arendt who said that.

What ruined these men?

Normative dissociation, says Jurgen Kremer, a German psychotherapist in the U.S. and author of E*thnoautobiography*.

These men disconnected from the land of their ancestors, their ancestors, the myths they used to live by, Nature, Community, history denied, dreams, spirituality and alienation from their own bodies.

The enlightenment era is blamed for this. But some will argue and say even in ancient civilizations, men were cruel. Not so fast…

All I know is that War is different from conflicts in indigenous cultures. In the latter the Earth speaks and instructs. Death is a natural part of the cycle of life. Balance is key.

Grief overcomes me when I think of wars all over the world instigated by a story that doesn't speak of Love, Balance, Humility.

Ontological Humility

Hauntological…

4.23.18

870 *I forgot the relief of witnessing a smile.*

And on the contrary, I am told that I should smile more or keep a smile on regardless of how one feels so that you don't look dour to others. Or in my case, intimidating. Suplada. Snob. Unapproachable.

I suppose there's something to this…it may have something to do with being a perfectionist Virgo—hard to please. Always the first thing to notice what's wrong with the world today.

I don't know where I get this. I am guessing it has to do with the fear of rejection. A common fear. Fear or lack of trust—people are out to get you, take advantage. Childhood sexual abuse trauma. Of things not being good enough. A restlessness of desire—of always wanting 'more' and 'better'.

What have I paid for? Unintended consequences of such learned attitude. Colonized eyes. Civilizational trauma.

What would recovery look like?
Living small. Living local.
Living minimally. Living with simple joy: gardening, meeting friends for coffee, sewing, playing the piano, mentoring young people. Giving money to causes.

No more tourist voyeurism.
No more escape to exotic destinations.
No envy of others who do.
No judgment of others who do.

4.24.18

590 *I forgot I painstakingly constructed a stage.*

A stage nudged by the dream of the round brown woman
Of underwater flights
Of apocalyptic dreams erasing my homeland from the map
Of clouds heavy with rain pouring a deluge and submerging a city
Of the cat kicked from a high rise and landing as a white tiger

All backdrops to the stage of a life that constructed me and not the other way around.

It is what happens when the depths of despair sink low enough to touch upon the dormant seeds in the womb of ancient mothers whose desires were unheard in the age of patriarchs.

The seeds sprout but with gnarled limbs and thin roots famished and threatening to shrivel up.

And the Earth noticed and sent Rain, Salt, Nutrients, Companion Seeds, Beneficial Insects—to guard the struggling seed until it was strong enough on its own.

This is the stage that constructed my life that became Ours.

4.25.18

537 I forgot strolling outside to hear trees murmur.

Trees murmur. Trees sing. Trees dance. Trees talk to us. Both science and indigenous knowledge agree on interspecies communication.

My intellectual work opened up to indigenous scholarship and there came a time when my body longed to experience this knowing that everything is alive and interconnected.

At Spring Lake a few years ago, I stopped to embrace an oak and a redwood tree. For the first time I felt the energy of each one: the oak's energy felt lighter and slow and flowing. The redwood tree's energy felt bold, solid, dense. I was surprised how good it felt to embrace the trees.

I have become a tree hugger!

My qi gong teacher taught us how to do an "embrace a tree" pose and hold it for 20 minutes while visualizing union with the tree and becoming aware of the life of the tree -- from her roots drawing water from the earth and warmth from the sun, nourishing her trunk, branches, leaves ...and then flowering, bearing fruit...in other words...the whole life cycle.

I am a Tree.

4.26.18

16 *I forgot the definition of childhood is ineffable.*

Ineffable = unspeakable; too much for words to carry.

And so it is. A childhood that is horrific and magical; innocent and brutal. Such contradictions take a lifetime to honor and forgive.

In the big house in Pampanga built in Spanish colonial design, we rented the basement. Before this, Mom and Dad and Ernie and Melinda lived at Eden Home— a dormitory run by Methodist missionaries. I think my Mom may have been the head of housekeeping. Dad was working at the U.S. military base.

When it was time for them to move they ended up in Indang Tamar's big house where she welcomed relatives to come and go as they pleased, stayed as they pleased.

In that house the old uncles were playing with us kids… at first innocently and then turning to sexual predation.

It was my Mom who saved us. She insisted on buying our own house, getting a loan to get us out of the house with monsters. I sensed that she may have had an inkling of what's going on and she wouldn't let her daughters be violated.

In our adult years, we shared stories of abuse and imagined those old men rotting in hell.

As for the lifetime impact of post-war trauma and childhood abuse, Ma and Tang made their way in the world supported by the missionaries and the church. Encouraging the straight and narrow walk of faith, we became disciplined in our pursuit of education, cosmopolitan sophistication, and religious devotion.

I no longer hate this past.
History has not taken anything from me.
I am still Stardust.

4.27.18

258 *I forgot the charisma of letters that formed words like myrrh, honey, balsam, pepper, wormwood—flavors used by Romans in Beaucaire to camouflage fermenting raisins spoiled in amphoras now lining the Mediterranean with thousands and thousands of shards.*

My gut reaction to this line is a *hhhmmmpphh!* I don't care about Romans and Mediterranean history or any of their so-called civilized, cosmopolitan airs borrowed from ancient cultures—whether Islamic or who knows…I am not really familiar with history in that part of the world.

In fact in this MDR, there are so many cultural references I am not familiar with or barely familiar. I am an island girl from the Pacific.

How do I unlearn the mimicry of colonizing cultures that made people like me feel inferior for so long? Ashamed of our brown skins and our earth-based spiritual cultures…

I do not need to mimic anyone or any culture supposedly superior. I am a learner and am an avid student of Life, of Big Ideas and so far modernity's big ideas are revealing themselves as hollow and toxic. We now know; so what is my responsibility in unlearning?

The idea of "catching up" with the West is traumatizing to so many of us. This is the anger that is erupting in violence—young people who took up the promise of progress, of 'better" only to be betrayed. Promises never meant to be kept.

How, indeed, do we unlearn?

4.28.18

421 *I forgot the room intimate with piano lessons.*

My mother, the piano teacher. The Luna family: violinist grandfather. The Joaquin Luna who created the UP Conservatory of Music. The Luna brothers—Antonio and Juan—artists, chemists, revolutionaries, politicians. National heroes.

My mom must have had quite a family. How else could she have learned how to play classical music? Why did we never get to ask her who her teachers were? I know she did mention taking lessons on the sly as she wasn't allowed because she is a girl.

We just took for granted that she could play Chopin, Bach, Beethoven, Debussy, Rachmaninoff. She made us all sit and learn to play the piano. And she had many students who loved her, especially the Methodist deaconesses.

The old German piano, repaired by Mr. Tongol, survived floods year after year. Was it a Steinway? I think it is still in the ancestral home.

My mother the pianist, the church pianist, the teacher.

Oh Mom, you were so quiet and didn't say much. And when I gave you journals for writing your stories, you said your memory is no good and what good does it do anyway to tell stories of years gone by?

I was wrong, Mom. I am so sorry. I will have to dream about you and I hope you can tell me stories that you want me to remember.

What would the piano say?

4.30.18

970 *I forgot how, once, you cracked. Even as your grip tightened, you whispered, "I am not as strong as you believe."*

The immediate image that arose from this line: You sitting across from me at dinner. I was lavishing You with praise for what I see as your "successful life"—wealthy, highly regarded government official, good father, good friend to many, etc.—and you said "things are not what they seem."

As I have projected this ideal onto you as a stand-in for the Homeland I left behind, I can see how I've longed for that ideal. I wanted it to be true but alas, my Homeland, you are an enigma.

On the surface, you have sacrificed much to catch up with the West. You cheer yourself with the billions of dollars in foreign remittance. Or the number of tourists who come to your pristine beaches and then ruin the environment. You have grand infrastructure ambitions as if you are a continent rather than a small island archipelago. You are self-destructing just like the rest of the planet.

And yet I still want to believe that you are strong. Resilient is how CNN describes you after each devastating typhoon.

No one, it seems, talks about climate change impacts so there are no preparations.

So there you are across the table from me smiling. I am nervous as I confessed the dreams I have of you where it's always the same question: why won't you love me?

Only to realize that I do not need to be loved.

I am Love.

4.30.18

62 I forgot a country somewhere, always at the opposite of where I stand on this earth.

"Over there are my islands," whispers the voice as I stand on Salmon Creek Beach in Northern California. This is where Apo Reyna Yolanda performed a ritual with about 20 of us in 2010.

Obeying her spirit guides, she said she needed to pray for safety as earthquakes are predicted.

For three hours we played (it felt like play) as she drew an image of the cosmos on the sand. She gave us instructions—jump, wave, hop, dance, look up—we followed even if we didn't understand what was going on. Her assistants simply said she's receiving instructions from the other realm.

Esoteric? Mystical? Play? It could be all of the above. Lesson learned: I will always be connected to the people and the land/Islands of that archipelago on the other side of Salmon Creek.

Such connections are so fragile. No longer romantic or exotic, no longer nostalgic—our connections perhaps have turned merely symbolic, ethereal, energetic connections.

Until the iron birds bring the friends bearing gifts from the land—banana chips with coco sugar, roselle tea, sampaguita oil…

And we touch, we taste, we smell.

All is alive again.

5.1.18

98 *I forgot you were the altar that made me stay.*

Who is my You? What's in my Altar? Where is the 'stay' place?

I sit in silence while I contemplate this You—and I call her by many names: Kwan Yin, Mary, Jesus, Buddha, Allah, Creator, Spirit, Ancestors, Angel, Energy, Consciousness, Self, Purusha.

In the vast cosmos, my life is an altar—because all is sacred. This altar can be called Poetry—if by Poetry is meant the language of Eros seeking to find its 'stay place', seeking Form for the Ineffable. Seeking sensuous connection that tingles the skin.

The 'stay place' is my Life… is a Home where we garden, where we raise chickens, where we read and sit, walk past neighbors' houses, cook and feed friends, house visiting guests, watch movies online…

This small place that is a refuge, a retreat place, a sanctuary for community.

You, who willed these into Being, you know what trickery you've played. What blessings bestowed. What tears have been shed. What pain has visited here.

It is all here.
An Altar to You

Long Life, Honey in the Heart (Martin Prechtel).

5.21.18

921 I forgot how, in all paths, branches wait without discrimination for someone's misstep.

Just got home from my university retirement party. In hindsight, I couldn't think of any missteps on my academic path. Instead I feel that my path has been ordained. I have been chosen to do what I've done. Often without being willful about it. From following prompts of spirit, fire in my belly that yearned for answers, looking for Home.

Tonight I saw how the branches have grown out of these inner promptings—creating containers for the unfolding of my students coming out of the cocoon of adulting and emerging as beautiful butterflies.

I loved hearing their stories of emergence, of decolonization, of loving themselves and loving their cultures. What can be more important?

We were Home again tonight, listening to stories of love, of community, of what's to come in the sacredness of it all.

5.4.18

659 *I forgot what was never called by a name.*

And without a Name
Without a Face
Without Language
What remains?

What is ineffable?
What if we all understood tacitly what this no-name is?
And we dance or sing around its presence?

Two indigenous students (Mohawk) were checking out a Colorado campus tour when they were booted out of campus because a parent who had become nervous had called the authorities because "the two were very quiet."

Here is Fear in the face of History—not ignorance, not incompetence on the part of school tour guides—this as the Shadow that swallows everything and creates another spectacle to be called out for public shaming in social media.

Perhaps it's good to call out such acts of unseeing
We want to see wrong made right
We want reconciliation
We want to see this collective trauma
Keep making it visible

5.1.18

3 I forgot why lovers destroy children to parse the philosophy of separation.

I am thinking of Noah tonight. At 13 he is changing fast—the little sweet boy turning into a little Dustin—brooding, quiet, intense—but maybe only when he is speaking with us via facetime. Maybe he is a social butterfly with his friends—as he seems to be busy sleeping over at a friend's' house or going to parties. I wonder what he is thinking.

I wonder how he is forming his opinions about Life, Love, Desire, Aspiration, Future. I wonder what he hears from his mom and dad. I wonder what questions he is too shy to ask.

I do not believe that children are immune to their parent's imperfections. But they will eventually form their own.

I wonder what he is learning from his peers, or the parents of his peers…from the culture of Fairfax, hippie town, liberal…

That is probably good. I hope he is learning something good—just like the song in *Wicked*: Because I knew you, I have been changed for good…

I, too, am changing for good as I learn something different at this time:
The way of the Earth
The way of Spirit
The way of Ancestors
The way of the Tao

5.6.18

10 *It was a different time. I forgot there is always a different time, even within the span of an hour (or less).*

Soon, I'll be referring to my academic life as belonging to a different time. But if I am to keep asserting that I am not a Time Being…and if I were to not talk about Time at all, what story will I tell?

I keep saying "Flow" these days referring to my experiences/my life as a gentle flow that has been carrying me all along like a river. Yes, I would like to keep this metaphor.

How does a River live her life? Sometimes she fights to breathe as she chokes on the toxic dumping from all sources—industrial wastes, human waste, chemicals…

In other places where she flows away from cities, she may be breathing a bit easier but if the source, like the Himalaya's melting ice caps, the downstream flow may not be enough to support the spawning of salmon.

I am River, too, flowing downstream. I have held canoes and fishing poles and kayaks and houseboats and rafts made of bamboo held together by rattan.

When Rain falls, the River swells and runs faster and rolls over and tumbles over. There have been times in my life when I felt the same way.

I've had dreams of floating down river on the back of a crocodile.

See when I don't think about Time, when I don't see thru Time, all these images come visiting wanting to befriend me.

Let the River flow.

5.7.18

127 I forgot the liberating anonymity conferred by travel: Mindanao, Berlin, Melbourne, Amsterdam, Istanbul became hours requiring no count.

Anonymity perhaps but some of my travels revealed parts of myself that haven't yet emerged. Like sitting at Parc Guell in Barcelona and realizing I'm a pilgrim paying homage to man-made cathedrals and castles in Europe which are all adorned with silk, marble, gold, silver taken from the colonies. What an awakening that was!

Or traveling to Mindanao when Duterte was Mayor in Davao and discovering that there are Filipinos who are more attached to Southeast Asia than Manila.

Or traveling by train to the Italian part of Switzerland and finding courage at being alone in a foreign country. Meeting other Filipinos in Geneva making lives, OFWs.

I would love to be anonymous in Peru, maybe Guatemala or Costa Rica, Brazil…I will not make it to these places I know.

Or Africa, India, China—parts of the world I will never see in person. I don't want to be a tourist.

Tourism as voyeurism
Tourism's huge carbon footprint

5.8.18

728 I forgot the ziggurat tattooed on an inner thigh, an area where inscription must have surfaced with anguish, then, desperation, then a hymn long forgotten as I'd forgotten how to attend anyone's church.

This line reminds me of the cultural practices that young Filipino Americans are appropriating in a good way, as they get in touch with their Filipinoness. Batok, Bangka, laga, and baybayin, kulintang, and other practices—all getting popular now and young entrepreneurs can even make a living out of products made.

I struggle with commodification especially when marketing strategies become sleek and trendy and visibly stylized to cater to a generation.

But I like that Lane Wilcken doesn't advertise, doesn't visibly talk too much. I like his seriousness and reverence of approach. I trust him.

These practices have created a community that is connected by thin slivers of thread of culture and ethnicity.

Such a thin line. Discernment is not easy.

But I know what my own path has been and where it has led me.

This small, local life. Tending a garden. Tending community.

A deepening diminishment…

5.9.18

849 *I forgot the difficulty of writing a poem, then turning it physical—I forgot its opposite is equally arduous…and lyrical.*

Either way, Poetry with words is difficult but Poetics as a way of Being is what I claim. I've always been in love with the idea of a Beautiful Life and how that looks like when your life is bare of accoutrements and full of angst and questioning and yet still manage to carve out a life that is meaningful and of service to a larger world beyond the personal.

I get teary eyed as I look back on my teaching life of 25 years in the U.S.—how it shaped a marriage, how it built a network, mycelia-like, with no known beginnings and endings—just a flowing with Eros—of finding a Source for one's idea of wholeness, of finding a place of Trust, of having Faith—different kinds of faith.

I watched *Dare to be Wild*—the story of Mary Reynolds who at 27 won the 2002 Chelsea Flower Show. A child who loved the wild and wanted it preserved forever—against all odds of finding the money to finance the costs of building her garden design and finding collaborators who understood her vision of the Wild…

Yes, it is possible to be Poetic even if you do not have the words to write a Poem.

Life is arduous enough.

5.10.18

566 *I forgot I knew better than to display flinch.*

Today I was tempted to flinch and become irritated, frustrated, lash out…but I didn't. I sense that the provocateur is feeling afraid, jealous, insecure and so she was going to try and get me to be on her side and rebuke her "enemy". She chided me for playing "favorites" in the community as if this perceived "favorites" was an affront to her.

So this is what it means to not forget what good leadership is, what emergent strategy can look like.

Creating a culture different from backstabbing, one-upmanship, groveling, obsequiousness, but to trust people (to know how to deal with their own mess) so they become trustworthy.

The Ocean doesn't flinch but if humans keep feeding her plastic she will belch and return what's been doled out to her.

Today at Bolinas beach with Lisa, I realized that kindness and generosity is the gift that keeps on giving.

5.11.18

590 *I forgot I painstakingly constructed a stage.*

Center for Babaylan Studies is that stage. I did not construct the stage by myself—there were Perla, Letecia, Baylan, Venus, Lizae, Mila, Frances, Lane, Lorial, Karen, Inday, Jen, Maileen, and countless volunteers. But, yes, in the programming I was primarily the person who visualized, made connections, and then created the stage for others to find their own path to decolonize and reindigenize.

In the process, we created a movement. We made connections. Nina Simons and Bioneers/Cultivating Women's Leadership was a big part of that because she introduced me to Tamalpais Trust. Made connections with Shailja Patel, Molly Arthur and many others.

The stage is virtual and non-local but I am often surprised that this stage has become an incubator for young people creating projects of their own. Finding their own voice and courage and creating their own networks of support. They are enlarging the circle.

Samantha Curl, Jo Cruz, Sammay Dizon, Jana Lynn Umipig, Jen Maramba, Nic Evans, Diyan Valencia, Lukayo Estrella—all carrying seeds and sowing them. Indigenous reclamation of cities, urban spaces.

Now I'm looking to Afrofuturism for more inspiration for post-academic work.

5.14.18

806 *I forgot Duende can overcome without satiating the* longing *for more.*

My inner Duende has overcome a lot of things for me: colonial mentality, internalized racism, classism, fundamentalism, fixed identities—all that were important as a path to decolonize. But overcoming—the constant struggle to be oppositional—is also limiting and sucks energy for other more creative pursuits.

Maybe this is why I am always attracted to artists who are pushing the envelope—not against (although that's always the context) but because their creative imagination births better scenarios than what is overcome.

I think it's a movement towards the proliferation of as many ideas as possible, or as many identities as possible—all working toward a shared responsibility to the Earth/ Land/Home.

So what is my *longing* now that I've overcome. My longing to be more generous, more kind, more hospitable, more open, more vulnerable, more willing to die to my stubborn ideas, more humble. I long to live small and local; to have a relationship with non-human beings even though I do not know how. I will learn to the extent that I can.

Duende, please listen to my longing.

Does overcoming mean letting go?

5.15.18

158 *I forgot the empty chair that awaited us, its expanse the totality of a planet still unexplored.*

I just ordered a book on Afro-futurism and *Octavia's Brood*, about visionary fiction. A way to imagine blackness outside the frame of a traumatic history and yet without leaving it behind but rather transmuting the past into the alchemy of a visionary future.

Like Wakanda in Black Panther.
Like *Parable of the Sower, Earth Seed, Kindred*

I looked up "Asiafuturism" and didn't find much to commend.

I want to find something on Pinayfuturism—who will imagine this? Who will create the future for us that is not about trying to "catch up" with the West or China or India.

We seem to forget that we are islands not continents. We are asked to dream big as if building malls and casinos owned by Chinese or owned by expats with Filipina wives is what would make us "better."

I am so tired of this story and yet I'm still at a loss to say something useful.

We always pride ourselves of our resilience, hospitality, caring, kapwa, bayanihan, kindness and yet we don't know how to explain extrajudicial killings, the murders of journalists and environmentalists.

Oh my homeland, I grieve and I refuse to go home to visit you.

Like a jilted lover, I have nothing to return to.

What is wrong with this picture?

5.22.18

650 *I forgot the dictator ending his reign as he began it: through deceit.*

Returning from CfBS Core Retreat where we learned about the rise of civilization and its unsustainability and the ideology of the sacred—the rationale created by the elites to pacify the masses into accepting the status quo; about trying to be indigenous in a fractured world.

"Was there a time period when we were fully human?" and if so, how is the genetic memory showing up in our lives?

I have no trust in dictators or in the so-called democratic governments that are merely masks for neoliberalism. Deceit becomes necessary to keep the system going.

But how then do we live in the system? How would emergent strategy help us change the way we relate to one another?

I see young Filipino Americans already practicing these strategies: kapwa in spirit and practice. Respectful of ancestors and traditions, creating new responses via food, music, dance, mixed media, murals, festivals.

Let the young ones lead.

What would elders do then?

What should the Center for Babaylan Studies (CFBS) do to prepare us for Elderhood?

5.23.18

1,162 *I forgot the radiance of darkness.*

What is dark right now is this one relationship with someone I cared about but that relationship has ruptured. I have no desire to suture it. Too hurt… wounded…traumatized.

I respected this person and supported the work she was doing. I created a platform for her so the world would know about her. She is a great artist. But when she publicly said that this very work that has supported her is not good enough because it was merely symbolic, then she lost me.

There is radiance in darkness.

The effect on me of this judgment is to pull back. This pulling back is also a calling in from my inner life—to take seriously what it means to be indigenous.

The Land where I now live, Pomo and Coast Miwok, called me to Dwell. The distancing from the homeland traditions is an effect or consequence of that. When the tradition is beleaguered to begin with and fractured—what can be done to mend it?

How quickly romance faded when I experienced disembodied presence.

This, too, is radiance in the darkness.

5.25.18

224 I forgot commitment costs.

I was committed to my liberation from the tyranny of colonial impositions. I gave three decades of my life to this project—arriving at the angle of repose—the acceptance of As Is and Just as It Is—and having now found my voice and power I use it to help others and support them in the same effort.

I am still committed to justice. I am committed to transformation.

Have there been costs?

I do not know. What have I sacrificed? What have I suffered? It's hard to answer these questions because they assume that something else was given up in the pursuit of this liberation. But I don't think I've given up or sacrificed much. Or lost anything. It's like Ilaya's question: Love or Duty? As if Love isn't also a Duty.

There's so much in the language that needs to change. We may not like dichotomy and yet we're always looking for an anchor, a ground to stand on in contrast to what we can't stand on.

So in this letting go of CfBS, I want to find an anchor that is Place-based...where my body is.

I do not feel the call to sit at a babaylan's feet in the homeland but I understand the need to support those who are wanting to do so.

5.25.18

*859 I forgot a girl singing forth her benedictions: May you never grow intimate with cold ashes and burlap. May you never feel tar and black feathers. May you know what I saw through...*flames.

I've come to believe that everyone on this planet has been infected with the virus of War—those who wage it may have rationalized it but they suffer the most.

Sometimes I feel like an alien. I can't relate to Hollywood and television, movies, sports, games, etc. It's not just age—it's the whole premise behind these.

I feel like the indigenous person brought out of the Amazon to the big city only to exclaim: *How can Mother Earth be repaid for all that's been taken from her to build this?*

I feel lost in this mirage.

And yet we still offer benedictions. And we offer a place for friends to commune and enjoy a home cooked meal. To sit around and laugh and to praise and to offer gratitude.

Benedictions for peace, for large-heartedness
For the overcoming of small hurts
For the judgment that is not ours to make
For the choice of releasing anger and worry
For the choice of having Joy as compass (Pat McCabe)

5.26.18

507 I forgot her hobby of attending death beds—afterwards, she always lusted for hotel lobbies stuffed with crystal chandeliers.

I sometimes wonder if every passion has two sides. Like being a death doula might be a passion but then to lust after crystal chandeliers in a hotel lobby is such a contrast. It reminds me of Ken Wilber who writes that once a year he would let go and go wild, do things he doesn't do on a regular basis.

This "letting go and going wild"—I wonder if this, too, is part of the illness of modernity. So tightly we wound ourselves over a passion that we lose balance and so the tightly wound life is released in ribaldry—overdrinking, bar life, spectacles, extreme sports—all in an attempt to unwind.

It doesn't make sense to me.

On the other hand, I wonder if my "balanced, slow, small, local life" is also teasing me into the extravagance of pleasures and surprises. Friends offering all kinds of ideas—to get drunk once in a while, to play golf, to do something that is not me, THC, ayahuasca—and I entertain the thought and then ask "why?"

What is there to run away from? Escape to?

Life is good as it is.

5.27.18

550 *I forgot intention is a form of focus, at times control.*

How has my intention/focus shifted recently?

This epiphany: Leny, you've spent most of your life resisting. You don't have to do that anymore!

So the focus is shifting—what does it mean to dwell in a place? What does it mean to claim an indigenous mind?

This gradual shift in intention/focus has affected my relationships with
— bookstores. I used to always find a book to buy but now I find not much to get excited about
— CfBS—letting go, allowing the next generation to lead
— local and small; nurture these relationships
— what is the best way to write and share?
— mentoring
— singing to the plants in the garden
— need to be in relationship with non-humans
— movies and tv—not interesting; news—mediocre
— travel. No to tourism.

Maybe as we cultivate this land-based life, we will be visited by people coming to see us.

The future of local projects—like Grief Retreat—and who knows what else will be born in our community.

We build community.

5.28.18

537 *I forgot strolling outside to hear trees murmur.*

When I decided that I was going to learn what it means to be indigenous I had to get over my prejudice against tree huggers. Stereotype of a white hippie, earth-loving, earth-serving, new ager. I always knew that when I'm critical of something, it's exactly what is calling me.

So one day as I walked around Spring Lake I decided to hug trees. The redwood is big and solid; with its straight trunk all the way to several hundred feet high, my arms wouldn't even reach around its girth/width but I lingered and felt the surging of energy. Buzzing, tingling, and co-mingling with my own energy. So this is what it feels like to fall in love with a tree!! Then I hugged a second tree—it might have been an oak—I should really find out for sure—this one has a different energy—it was softer, smoother, gentle—I could tell the difference between the two.

Since then I've hugged the apricot and apple trees in our garden. I talk to them when I'm sad. Sometimes I would just sit on the ground and my back against her trunk.

Andreas Weber speaks of this biology of enchantment and enlivenment—to begin to understand that all these non-human beings have a desire to be alive and to be in relationship with us; that our own identity is bound up in this reciprocal relationship.

It is real and I am growing this experience day by day.

5.29.18

67 I forgot abandoning misery until it became mere concept; then poem.

Not too long ago, I was driving home from the fitness place and this voice said: You've spent most of your life resisting. You don't have to do that anymore. You can just be. You are enough.

The voice was like a bell—crystal and clear. Unbidden. I wasn't particularly thinking of anything related to the message.

But this voice transformed me. It's as if I am being given a new way of being in the world—not as postcolonial, decolonizing, anti-imperialist, anti-capitalist, anti-patriarchy—that by just Being who I am with my Kapwa, I am a conduit for the message of Beauty and Wholeness.

Yes, the 30s, 40s were miserable years—full of angst, anger, frustration with this culture of whiteness and I've made my way out of it now.

I am finding others who are walking out of academe, out of toxic relationships, out of corporate jobs, and creating/crafting a life that is based on gift giving and sharing.

This is the culture we come from—that has been lost in the process of being colonized and racialized—and we can reclaim it.

Not in the name of saving the planet or going to heaven but simply because this is how Love thrives.

BE.

5.30.18

103 *I forgot how one begins marking time from a lover's utterance of farewell.*

2007: Koan appears
2008: Koan disappears

Koan reappears in my dream except this time he is saying goodbye and turns into a tree.

What is the dream's message? I thought I've figured it out but it turns out that I still haven't. The Homeland says: I will always love you. But I have to go for now. Remember that I love you.

So perhaps this dream has given me permission to say farewell temporarily so I can focus on my settler work and dwelling. To learn what "indigenous" means as a relationship with land, community, and family—this has been my work.

The podcast interviews of Rochelle, Bayo, and Erin speaks of this transition. But what does it mean in terms of looking ahead?

Every morning I tend to the body and then spend time with Cal. A part of me is looking for a more enlivened existence.

I am thinking of traveling to the homeland but when?

6.4.18

351 *I forgot to be an angel is to be alone in a smudged gown, fingers poking through holes burnt by epistemology.*

Makes me smile — this image of an angel, alone, in a smudged gown…

Her fingers poking through holes burnt by epistemology, a Greek concept.

How do you know what you know?—it's actually more of a Koan. But the rational mind would squeeze all of its reasons to arrive at an answer—brain cells at work.

Preferably an objective one, reduced to its essence, irrefutable if possible

A gown must be smudged but I don't think it means to be made sacred—as when in indigenous ceremony we smudge to keep bad spirits away. Smudge on the other hand is to smear, to make dirty, and unattractive.

Let's poke holes in this gown burnt by epistemology—how would Vizenor turn this around like a trickster of unreason; how would Coyote do this?

Epistemology is languishing these days as we invent new languages and imagine new worlds that doesn't count on White Supremacist Capitalist Patriarchy (WSCP) values that honors the Earth—

Hylozoism
Chthulene
Postanthropocene
Posthumanist
Rhizomatic
Newmaterialistfeminist

Why can't we simply say:

Water is Life
Mni Wiconi
Kapwa
Ginhawa
Damdamin

6.7.18

956 I forgot the aftermath from dilemmas of belonging.

God is change.
All that you touch, you change; changes you. (Octavia Butler)

The question of Belonging changes over a lifetime. In the beginning of my sojourn to the U.S., belonging was a longing that can only be filled with returns to the homeland. Belonging happened only in glimpses of encounters with kapwa; with letters and emails from home.

Belonging slowly shifting from belonging to an ethnic and cultural group to a feeling you cultivate in yourself—a resolve to understand the roots of alienation. Finding a story big enough to contain your multitudes and paradoxes.

Belonging became a question of belonging to the Source and Original Instructions. Vedanta meditations were helpful but too abstract and needed to be grounded in Place.

Belonging is the work of embodiment—when the Earth is your body—when the universe is in you—when your breath is the breath of all Life.

Belonging is knowing this in your body—connection with the Earth and Cosmos—all beings are alive and looking for relationship.

Belonging is a state of awareness and presence—healing of all we have been disconnected from as we became modern.

Belonging is a trust relationship. Even as we tiptoe to the edge of the abyss—our elegant disintegration and disappearance is welcome.

6.8.18

861 *I forgot Heaven could be…a breath away I forgot why a girl remained in song.*

Anthony Bourdain died by suicide today at 61. There is a rise in suicides in the USA among the youth, 15-34.

There is an atmosphere of despair that is covered over, or looked away from and there is plenty that distracts us: NBA finals, Go Warriors!, tv spectacles, tv pundits, etc. This is a country that knows how to drown itself in opioids, spectacle, binge drinking…

And at the same time there are burgeoning spiritual communities everywhere—even in yoga studios, meditation centers, transformation festivals, concerts.

These are all organized, curated events that bring people together but people then go back to their apartments. No emotional connection in isolation. No community. Malnourished emotionally, bereft of connections that go deep in the bone marrow capable of sustaining us in our aloneness.

Kapwa is this strong impulse that, if deepened and nurtured with attention, listening, and being present, may mean giving up other parts or preoccupations. But we must make time.

Which reminds me that I must make time for my girlfriends…

6.8.18

621-645 *I forgot my father is not....*

These are all names of dictators, murderers, ethnic cleansers—who ruined their peoples or attempted to...

Patriarchy's reign is bloody terror and a lot is to be blamed for.

Many offer the Feminine as an antidote but even this, I think, might be dangerous unless it is clearly rooted in Place/Land and in indigenous paradigms.

How do we build and live the future now? There are more and more people thinking about this and they all say the same: Local and Small scale economies and communities = shifts in consciousness = shifts in practice and daily habits and consuming patterns = all of which will begin to shift the culture.

Regina drove me to SF today and she wanted to connect; she's learning to be a healer and I wonder if she has a mentor and is developing her spiritual life.

It is good to witness the events in San Francisco at today's Kapwa mural project.

6.10.18

583 *I forgot eyes widening to pull in more of the world.*

But then what do you do when you take in the world and become overwhelmed and discouraged by the anthropocene era and its hubris? Some would say this is part of the process of the cosmos dying, decaying, rebirthing, recycling, expanding, appearing, disappearing.

We are not used to grieving or witnessing these processes from a post-human, post-activist, new materialist lens. We aren't used to imagining outside-the-box perspectives.

This afternoon I watched videos of rich Asians from China spending and buying up Vancouver, Australia—sending daughters to college in the U.S.—going to City College driving Lamborghinis, buying up condos and real estate. The locals couldn't afford to compete.

Chinese capitalists descending on America.

Americans, on the other hand, are leaning to the East via spiritual traditions, Buddhism, Taoism, meditation, qi gong, yoga, acupuncture, Vedanta, kirtans…

I've always said this: someday the West will become spiritual and the East will become more materialist.

Yin
Yang
Either way it will not stop the advance of climate crisis.

6.11.18

421 *I forgot the room intimate with piano lessons.*

Mother's piano went with us in every house we moved to…well, actually only in two houses. The first wasn't even a house—it was the first floor of a Spanish style house which we rented until my mother decided to buy our own home—a nipa hut to start with that we kept adding on to until it became a rambling house like Howl's moving castle…and after many years of floods and mud we finally tore it down and built a modern bungalow which actually hasn't served us well in the era of more floods and volcanic ash flows.

The piano lived thru these times. Today I play the piano when I remember my Mom and how she made us all sit and learn; a most civilizing way I suppose. We became good at it. In fact so many Filipino and Asian parents have their kids take up an instrument—violin, cello, flute, clarinet, piano—a measure of sophistication and cosmopolitan taste to show off.

Even now I once in awhile miss the days when we had concerts in the living room. The Mendoza sisters rehearsing Broadway tunes to perform at Masonic events or at church.

Somehow we drifted away from those days and now I often think of how to integrate the history of those moments to reconcile the paradox of being colonized and decolonized all at once.

6.12.18

320 *I forgot unfamiliarity with the edges of my body.*

In Dance I become aware of my body—from my toes to the top of my head. And then the Breath. The energy rising from the Earth, the sun/Cosmos coming down thru the Bai Hui.

The energy body, the physical body, the emotional body—all these systems dancing, vibrating.

I've always wondered what 'raising your vibration' means—if it simply means when you can love everything then your vibration is high. If you stumble across something you hate or dislike then it lowers your vibration.

Oh dear. Doesn't this sound like new age talk? But then listen to biologists and physicists talking about microbiomes and every wave particles, quantum physics—it all comes alive!

Or when in Qi Gong practice you start to feel the tingling in your fingers and then your whole body starts to feel warm and tingly.

In the moment of concentration and focus, I can tune in.

I danced with Carolyn again today—she's so open and brimming with vitality—and love of everything, everyone.

She inspires me.

6.13.18

371 I forgot 'mutual funds' is an oxymoron.

I did not know anything about mutual funds until I started making money and was asked to invest my savings in a mutual fund. Of course, it wasn't really mutual because the finance guy was more interested in his commission than in growing my portfolio. We trusted that he understood our concern about socially responsible investing but in the end, we lost some funds and he was eventually fired.

Anyway, the banking and finance world is a big bubble that will collapse eventually... as all economies eventually do—in a revolution, in a natural catastrophe—but it will be a slow one—so slow that even if we know it's coming, the systems in place will have a hard time transitioning.

There are lots of talk about it—post capitalist, post anthropocene, post humanist, post this and that signaling what is emerging in the shadow of our slow demise.

Scientists, conservationists, philosophers, artists, indigenous elders, scholars—whichever way you look, there's always someone willing to sell Hope.

Hope without the mandate to change the world view—neoliberalism, freedom, democracy, etc—all these ideologies have failed the majority of peoples on the planet and yet we keep the evening news keyed in to the stock market as if that's all it boils down to.

Bahala Na you say but unless you attach this to something more tangible, it rings hollow—and its promise empty: the tyranny of Hope.

6.15.18

246 *I forgot generous beds of unpicked mint—radically fragrant but untapped potential.*

A lot of suburban gardeners like the idea of planting and buying potted plants at the nursery to transplant in the garden. Voila, instant results! They put in veggie starters and then six to eight weeks later, the tomatoes, zucchini or whatever else needs harvesting are left unharvested and rotting on the ground.

Sometimes I'm tempted to steal oranges, pineapple guavas, tomatoes, artichokes, from other people's gardens that are neglected.

I say it is not kind to the fruit or nut tree to give so much of their babies and then to be ignored or left alone to rot and fall.

Yes, of course, what falls to the ground is composted back to soil but sometimes people hire those gardeners who vacuum everything or blow everything into the sidewalk. I always abhor these noisy leaf blowers.

Yes, mint unpicked will continue to spread and take over the garden.

So make tea, make oil, make salads, put in Vietnamese fresh egg rolls.

All takes time.

Must slow down.

6.16.18

295 *I forgot part of mortality's significance is that wars end.*

Wars will end when humans are wiped off the face of the earth. Or maybe not all humans—only the baby boomer generation who is supposedly responsible for this modernity's eventual demise.

They've all had their fill of malls stuffed with goods sourced around the world.

Wars are fought over resources even though the master narrative never says it. Wars are fought by the USA to protect "the American lifestyle" that needs endless supply of oil, water, minerals, silk, cotton, labor…

Wars are fought because of the fear of Death and denial of it. The promise of limitlessness, of eternal life, of a reward in heaven, of "you can be whatever you want to be"—of all of these promises cannot be fulfilled in one lifetime. Other things happen in life.

Suffering happens.

Grief happens.

Balance Grief and Gratitude.

6.17.18

956 I forgot the aftermaths from dilemmas of belonging.

In Vedanta this sense of belonging is Awareness itself. When the mind is skillful enough to know the difference between person and Self, you know Belonging in its truest sense.

All else is prakriti—the mind's never ending proclivity for drama.

Today I was sucked into the dramas of an incident that hasn't resolved itself. I am not feeling compelled to initiate a path to reconciliation. It is not my responsibility to do so. So much better to let it be.

Sad, yes, but not much I can do.

Who do I want to belong to these days? And how is today's desire different from yesterday's?

Yesterday's desire was about the attraction to learn about Indigenous Peoples in the Philippines and about my own ancestral roots—and these have been answered already in a way that is satisfactory to me.

My roots might be settler/colonizer all the way down. I am not Aeta. I am probably ethnic Chinese/Malay or Pacific Islander. I am also Spanish. I am hybrid. Kapampangan recorded history begins with the Spanish era.

So for folks like me, claiming a sense of belonging settles for the present and dwelling in a place with integrity and respect for those whose land was stolen and must be returned.

Hybridity is a slippery concept and I don't know if I'd settle for it so easily.

Settlers recovering indigenous mind is okay. It is a process that is ongoing. Hopefully a worthwhile one.

I have no desire to do gatekeeping.

6.18.18

442 I forgot the deceit in conclusions.

The age of Certainty is over. The age of Reason is over. The age of Anthropocene is over. Now the debris left over by these master narratives is being gathered by the next generation. They intend to shred the template and do things differently. But their version of 'different' is really a harkening back to a time when the people were hunter-gatherers, animists, who understood their symbiotic relationship with all the beings and the Land they lived in. It's said that a band of about 150 is the ideal size for a community to be able to move around easily as they follow food, seasons, plants, animals.

Hundred of thousands of years of observation, presence, participatory consciousness sharpened their skills that have made them survive today.

I love how a Pomo friend responded to a friend's rant against environmentalists who wouldn't let him save the beloved abalones on the Sonoma Coast. Even invoking the fate of indigenous peoples who have always relied on abalone for food—my friend gently and sweetly simply reminded the abalone lover of what has been forgotten, devalued and now here we are suffering the consequences of forgetting.

Her gentle response softened his as well—being reminded that Time is not the culprit here, nor is it the environmentalists at fault and other figures.

People have forgotten their relationship with the Land, Ocean, Earth. We must find our way back.

6.19.18

103 *I forgot how one begins marking time from a lover's utterance of* Farewell.

Today is Jose Rizal's birthday. I just thought I'd mention it even though it doesn't feel particularly poignant or nostalgic because to many ordinary folks who didn't get their history lesson on national heroes indelibly etched in memory—his birthday passes as unremarkable and that is sad.

Rizal is said to have had lovers whose hearts he broke. And how did the firing squad that ended his life as a martyr for his people's independence also mark a lover's farewell to his beloved?

I haven't had many lovers and only two farewells I would mark as momentous. When I said goodbye to R because I started to date someone else, he merely laughed at me as if Love ends or has an ending. It doesn't. I know that now.

The other goodbye with B was more dramatic as it involved having to explain to him and his wife the meaning of Eros vs Romance and how capitalist systems discipline Love and confines it to the monotony of monogamy. It was so silly of me to try to convince them both. In my dreams soon after, he was always saying goodbye and promising a love beyond goodbye.

May all our Lovers be beyond Farewells. Love never ends. In Love there is no Time. In Love we are not Time beings.

6.20.18

98 *I forgot you were the altar that made me stay.*

What are the altars we've created to enshrine our deepest desires, longings, prayers for a life well lived?

In one room I have a painting by Potenza called "Blessed are Women". There's a retablo made by my son in honor of my mother. Two Shona sculptures—Emerging Woman and Proud Girl—at one time represented my inner self trying to find a voice. A statue of Kwan Yin, a photo of Inanna and other gifts given to me by friends and kindred spirit honoring the sacred.

In the living room is an altar to my parents and grandmother, an eagle feather and braided sweetgrass from Haines Makes Noise, a Lakota elder and friend. Betel nut, precious stones, petrified wood, and again gifts from friends.

What do these represent? What story do they say of where I've stayed for 35 years in a suburban tract home?

Who are You that holds me in this place, providing Anchor and Refuge. Haven for a community that has grown together.

I have stayed for You! And created an Altar of a Place to honor this Call to my restless spirit. I have not always been willing to surrender. I have not always been willing to let go of attachment. But slowly I am beginning to notice that mindfulness is leading me here just the same. In spite of Me.

And as always—what begins as an adventure of the intellectual life becomes a vessel for a more poetic life and way of being.

6.21.18

113 *I forgot admiring women who refuse to paint their lips.*

I am envious of women who do not wear any makeup, can go out in public, looking bare and still get away with it. I mean—when I go out in public without make up—I am often treated poorly by customer service folks who project their stereotypical attitudes on me.

Every year I tell myself that I will no longer line my eyes, shape my eyebrows, color my lips and I always break my promise.

But during the firestorm I did just that for two weeks—too anxious and worried to be vain. We were all refugees for two weeks in temporary shelters.

I wonder if the cosmetic industry will ever go bankrupt when women refuse to wear makeup, whiten their skin, sculpt their noses, tighten their sagging skin, etc.—all the things we do to feel attractive. Some of it is instinct I suppose. The need to attract mate—the way birds primp themselves to call a mate.

I wish Beauty is intrinsic. Where we see the divine in each other. Beautiful just as we are.

But I have a hard time visualizing this when I think of children who are taken away from their parents.

The hardening of hearts.

The turning of our eyes and ears to sorrow.

The silence as a look.

Afraid, afraid

6.22.18

387 *I forgot authenticity always wanders.*

What is the opposite of wander then? Of staying? Rooted? Grounded? Not likely to disappear without goodbye? Of loyalty? Commitment to a vow?

What is given up when we settle? When we give up wandering in search of an elusive and ineffable answer to a Koan? I think this, too, is the romance promised by modernity—the perpetual wanderer as an adventure seeker, risk taker, explorer of the unknown, always searching for a newness that turns on the hormones of excitement and the rush of a spectacle.

A whole culture is like this—all the wanderers have ruined nearly every corner of this Earth. Having no sense of responsibility and accountability and no relationship to the Earth as living being, other creatures having their own legitimate claim to Be— the human species have made a mess of things in the name of an authenticity that is based on a civilizational turn that desacralized the Earth.

Now we know. I know that maybe there is no turning back on this story. Not in my lifetime anyway. But how do I want to live the rest of my time here?

Everyone asks me where I'm going to wander next. The questions sadden me. Yet if I talk back what would come back to me?

And it feels the same as I did 25 years ago when I first raised my voice to be heard against the grain.

6.24.18

1,017 *But I will never forget we walk on the same planet and breathe from the same atmosphere. I will never forget the same sun shines on us both. I created my own legacy.* No one is a stranger to me.

I was just reading Mary Oliver's essay on the loneliness of the creative life and the self as the worst critic and saboteur of the creative life.

How we always find an excuse not to do the most creative work asked of us.

I know this is true for me. I play games on my phone, watch Bollywood movies on Netflix. I go to the gym, go for a walk, cook, spend too much time on FB—because I don't always know how to create the space where I can speak and be heard.

Sometimes I think no one reads anything anymore that is longer than a meme or a headline.

Our attention spans have shrunk. Shouldn't I be worried about all these things?

Sure, life will be more challenging in the USA—but why shouldn't it when the rest of the planet is suffering as well?

We are changing; we are unlearning; we are undoing—all the things/values that did us in—greed, competition, individualism, "I don't care"—between leaving old ways and habits of thinking and doing and learning new ones.

It feels unsettling.

I don't want to feel as if I'm bypassing spiritually.

No one is a stranger to me—not even those who are not in love with the Earth as Mother. They may love the idea of a Father God in Heaven who has given them permission to treat everything as an object of desire.

6.25.18

1,167 *I forgot my poetry is going to change the world. I forgot my words are healing. I forgot my words are apples infused with cheerful cinnamon. I forget my words are holy. I forgot my words are going to lift you—all of you! towards Joy!*

This is the last line in MDR and the last line to close this journal exercise.

It grieves me to forget
        that words are Holy
                are Healing
                    will change the World
        will lift towards Joy

It grieves me that we have forgotten—in the midst of this march towards fascism in this country—that Joy, Beauty—is the healing we need right now.

May we remember the suffering and the sacrifices of women, mothers, slaves, children who have given their lives to causes greater than themselves.

The native peoples who have survived with dignity and tricksterish humor are showing us that empires, dictators, tyrants will never last.

May we remember the Beauty of the small and local movements that sustain communities.

May we remember the songs, especially the lullabies, that mothers sang to calm their babies.

May we remember the poems phrases, the images gifted to us by poets, painters, dancers, visionaries.

Remember! Remember!

I close this journal with the happy memories of James Corden and Paul McCartney's carpool karaoke.

As a kid I loved Paul and learned the early Beatles' songs—they must have carried me through my teen years and beyond.

So I leave you with

IMAGINE

APPENDIX 1

MURDER DEATH RESURRECTION: A Form of Babaylan Poetics

The Foreigner in My Blood

I forgot any reason for you to hold my hand as a day unfolded
I forgot how your eyes always reached for me when I passed the threshold into the home we carefully shared
I forgot memory's fragments which deserve to be the ones in the forefront of my attention
I forgot how my mother chastised, "Your grandmother's home may be meager to Western eyes. But, once, it housed invading generals waving foreign flags."

I felt a tingling as I wrote down these lines last night. It felt uncanny, maybe even a bit eerie. I chose the numbers of my birthdate — 9+11+19+52 to generate a poem from Eileen Tabios' MURDER DEATH RESURRECTION or MDR, project's 1,167 lines. I did it for the second time; this time using my son's birthdate — 3+11+19+72:

Sometimes Love Laments

I forgot why lovers destroy children to parse the philosophy of separation
I forgot how your eyes always reached for me when I passed the threshold into the home we carefully shared
I forgot memory's fragments which deserve to be the ones in the forefront of my attention
I forgot fingertips smoothed to black velvet from constantly rolling leaves of tobacco.

On the sideline of my notebook, I had put exclamation marks on the first and fourth lines of the second poem because they speak to a literal truth. Again, I was seized by a bemused and awed feeling…something almost akin to the incredulity of the rational mind that refuses to bend to the seduction of the mysterious. But I know that lurking in the shadow of my psyche is a curiosity and affection for that which is hiding from my plain sight. Poetry always does that for me.

I have friends who believe in numerology, astrology, tarot readings and other similar phenomena. My interest in same is peripheral to this day because, while I find it fascinating, I haven't really delved into these things studiously.

However, I have been reading Arnold Mindell's books on transpersonal psychology, processwork, social change and spirituality. When he writes about "second attention or secondary reality" I resonate loudly with the concept because this speaks to the intuitive way I have carved out a path for myself that turned into an academic career/vocation. This is also at the heart of the methodology of Pagtatanung-tanong (literally asking questions repeatedly) in <u>Filipino Indigenous Psychology</u>. This methodology is embedded within the concepts of <u>KAPWA (shared self)</u> and <u>LOOB (shared</u> humanity).

Filipino scholar on indigenous philosophy, <u>Fr. Albert Alejo</u> writes that the concept of Loob is similar to the <u>concept of the TAO</u> in Asian philosophy. I don't have the space here to expound on the comparisons of these concepts but those who are familiar with Taoist philosophy may have a tacit understanding of what it means to flow in the way of the Universe, to be in process, to being in "Wu Wei"—no forceful action.

All the above comes to mind as I engage Eileen Tabios' latest book, <u>Murder, Death Resurrection</u>—a poem that is 1,167 lines long culled from 27 of her earlier poetry books. She explains that the "murder" comes from putting to death these earlier works, so to speak, so that she may resurrect them into new forms. She assumes that a reader can select any number of these lines and the result would be a new poem.

She has faith, she says, the new poem will be aesthetically pleasing to the reader who engages the Generator because she believes in the practice of <u>Babaylan poetics.</u> Eileen is the only poet I know who is audacious enough to claim this power. Babaylan—the precolonial figure of the shaman, medicine woman, healer, folk therapist, chanter, ritualist, mediator with the spirit world in the Philippines—has long been buried in the cultural memory of modern Filipinos in the homeland and in the diaspora. But this hidden figure is also being resurrected by the <u>Center for Babaylan Studies</u>. Since 2009, the Center has offered conferences, symposia, retreats, workshops, books and other publications, projects supporting indigenous communities in the Philippines and in the diaspora—all in the spirit of wanting to Enliven us again, heal our colonial wounds, and return us to the Beauty of our indigenous heritage.

English has wounded me/us. In spite of my academic creds, I am acutely aware of how English limits me and how my native tongues (Kapampangan and Tagalog) would prefer to chant or sing than theorize; or how my body would prefer to do meditative qi gong than bend my brain trying to explain in English what my bones already carry and understand.

So in a way these "I forgot" poems rescue my imagination and allow me to appreciate English; perhaps be more tender towards my self's distance from it. In the hands of a soulful and skillful poet like Eileen, these poems can be the vessel of Beauty.

Babaylan poetics is a practice in immanence and transcendence for me. In the CfBS circle, we claim our Babaylan-inspired indigenous spirituality that manifests itself in the forms that we create as a community of scholars, activists, healers, teachers, artists, culture-bearers who are learning how to decolonize and re-indigenize. Spirit/ Creator/God/Tao/Loob is not some external heaven-ward presence that we invoke when in need; this Presence is in our midst in all forms, human and non-human, seen and unseen. Poems, too, when born out of faith and trust in the flow of the Tao, bear the mark of the Babaylan spirit's presence.

This Presence is also in the cover of Eileen's book that bears Pacita Abad's art work. Babaylan poetics begins in the cover page…and before that and beyond. It is all connected.

As for the lines above in "The Foreigner in my Blood", I am reminded of how entangled I already am with my "others" and everyday is a practice in honoring these relationships and making no room for spiritual bypassing when it gets challenging.

So sometimes Love Laments but Love Always Is. That is Babaylan Poetics. That is Kapwa.

https://medium.com/@lenystrobel/murder-death-resurrection-a-form-of-babaylan-poetics-df6caadbddd3

ABOUT THE AUTHOR

Leny Mendoza Strobel is Professor Emeritus of American Multicultural Studies at Sonoma State University. She is also one of the Founding Directors of the Center for Babaylan Studies. Her books, journal articles, online media presence reflect her decades-long study and reflections on the process of decolonization and healing of colonial trauma through the lens of indigenous perspectives. She is a grandmother to Noah and she tends a garden and chickens with Cal in Northern California. More information is available at https://www.lenystrobel.com/.

Established in 2016, **PALOMA PRESS** is a San Francisco Bay Area-based independent literary press publishing poetry, prose, and limited edition books. Paloma Press believes in the power of the literary arts, how it can create empathy, bridge divides, change the world. To this end, Paloma has released fundraising chapbooks such as *MARAWI*, in support of relief efforts in the Southern Philippines; and *AFTER IRMA AFTER HARVEY*, in support of hurricane-displaced animals in Texas, Florida and Puerto Rico. As part of the San Francisco Litquake Festival, Paloma proudly curated the wildly successful literary reading, "THREE SHEETS TO THE WIND," and raised money for the Napa Valley Community Disaster Relief Fund. In 2018, the fundraising anthology, *HUMANITY*, was released in support of UNICEF's Emergency Relief campaigns on the borders of the United States and in Syria.

CPSIA information can be obtained
at www.ICGtesting.com
Printed in the USA
FSHW011833280719
60480FS